W9-BIZ-739

THE UNCONVENTIONAL INVENTION BOOK

by

Bob Stanish

Illustrated by **Nancee Volpe**

Copyright © Good Apple, Inc., 1981

ISBN No. 0-86653-035-5

Printing No.   15 14

The purchase of this book entitles the buyer to duplicate the student activity pages as needed, for use by students in the buyer's classroom. Permission for any other use must be granted by Good Apple, Inc.

GOOD APPLE, INC.
BOX 299
CARTHAGE, IL 62321

All rights reserved. Printed in Hamilton, IL USA by Hamilton Press, Inc.

Acknowledgements

The author wishes to thank the D.O.K. Publishing Company for permission to reprint the SCAMPER techniques, from SCAMPER, by Bob Eberle. Additional acknowledgements to:

      Bob Eberle, consultant and author, Edwardsville, IL

      Mary Henri Fisher, Director, Gifted Program Section, Superintendent of Public Instruction, Olympia, WA

      Marge Frank, consultant and author, Deerfield, IL and Ashland, OR

      Cheryl Millar, Illinois State Board of Education, Program Services Team, Springfield, IL

for their assistance along the way.

      and to:

      Joe Renzulli, professor, The University of Connecticut at Stoors, for his Foreword,

      and to:

      Todd Christensen, teacher, Maple Park Elementary, Lynnwood, WA

      Kathy Hagen, teacher, Auburn School District, Auburn, WA

      Joanne Hess, teacher, Franklin Pierce School District, Tacoma, WA

      Karen Kale, teacher, Ellensburg School District, Ellensburg, WA

      Glenna Matson, teacher, Lake Washington School District , Kirkland, WA

      Micki McKisson, teacher, Issaquah School District, Issaquah, WA

      Kate Mortenson, teacher, Educational Service District, Spokane, WA

      Sharon Sell, teacher, Central Valley School District, Spokane, WA

      Roberta VanderSluis, teacher, Oak Harbor School District, Oak Harbor, WA

      Gary Westcott, teacher, Evergreen School, Seattle, WA

      Jan Zuber, teacher, Bellevue School District, Bellevue, WA

for their field testing of the activities.

Foreword

Classroom teachers are always on the lookout for activities that will develop inventive thinking skills, and the collection that follows is a gold mine for such activities. The book provides thorough and easy-to-follow teacher's guides and offers hundreds of suggestions about how to accommodate inventive and creative thinking in a variety of classroom projects and instructional approaches. The work sheets are "ready-to-use" and delightfully illustrated. But, what is more important is the fact that almost all of the activities are open-ended, and they therefore allow each child to "escalate" his or her level or response in these highly imaginative thinking exercises.

There are several advantages to the activities included in this book in addition to the primary benefits mentioned above. Youngsters are provided with an opportunity to express themselves through creative drawing as well as creative thinking and writing. The author has also provided excellent suggestions for varying the activities so that each activity, in effect, represents a takeoff point for the classroom teacher to develop additional related activities of his or her own. This feature is an especially important one because it encourages classroom teachers to develop their *own* creative thinking abilities and in this manner to serve as a model for creative thinking rather than merely someone who just talks about it. The author also offers suggestions for warm-up activities and ideas for following through on each lesson. This approach again helps to extend the content of the book.

THE UNCONVENTIONAL INVENTION BOOK will serve as an excellent resource for any classroom teacher who is interested in providing a wide variety of stimulating experiences for all kinds of kids. The many stimulating ideas included in this book will bring many hours of learning and enjoyment to both students and teachers.

Joseph S. Renzulli
Professor of Educational Psychology,
The University of Connecticut

DEDICATION

This book is dedicated to:
snowflakes,
hot air balloons,
and magic dragons.
I saw them all through my
classroom window.

CONTENTS

BEFORE YOU BEGIN...

What This Book Is All About *1*

What's in the Book *1*

How to Use This Book *2*

PART I: The Nuts and Bolts of Unconventional Inventing *4*

What Is Inventive Thinking? *5*

How to Generate Student Inventiveness *8*

References *20*

Bibliography *21*

PART II: Making the Unconventional Conventional *24*

Activity No. 1 .... *26*

Activity No. 2 .... *28*

Activity No. 3 .... *30*

Activity No. 4 .... *32*

Activity No. 5 .... *34*

Activity No. 6 .... *36*

Activity No. 7 .... *38*

Activity No. 8 .... *40*

Activity No. 9 .... *42*

Activity No. 10 .... *44*

Activity No. 11 .... *46*

Activity No. 12 .... *48*

PART III: The Unconventional Invention Activities *50*

A Few Teaching Tips for Using the Unconventional Invention Activities *51*

Bug Crunchers *52*

Dress Some Friendly Aliens *54*

Happy Cups *56*

Unhang a Coat Hanger *58*

Special Delivery *60*

Aid a Gator *62*

Car Wash *64*

Name Quilts *66*

Redesign the Human Body *68*

Vegetables and Things *70*

Force-Fitting Functions *72*

Out of Sight *74*

Similar Opposites *76*

Design a Cycle 78

"I" Chart 80

The Untold Story 82

Improve a Smile 84

A Bad-Taste Detector 86

A Look Inside 88

Design a Playground 90

Stretch a Doughnut 92

Things Within Things 94

Luv 96

What a Name! 98

Reversing Myself 100

This Is My Bag 102

Scroodles 104

Field Goal Machine 106

Suction Critter 108

Color My Speech 110

PART IV: Lesson Planning for Inventive Thinking 112

PART V: Unconventional Invention Patent 120

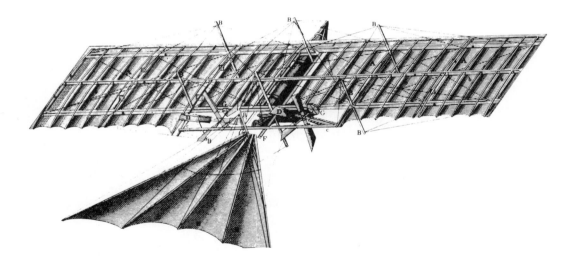

Before you begin.....

What this book is all about:

THE UNCONVENTIONAL INVENTION BOOK is for developing student inventiveness and originality. Its major function is to cause students to BE DELIBERATELY CREATIVE.

What's in the book:

The book consists of FIVE PARTS:

PART I: THE NUTS AND BOLTS OF UNCONVENTIONAL INVENTING.

This section contains the whys, the wherefores and the how-to-do-its. There are numerous ideas in this section that can be used in conjunction with the book's activities, or in conjunction with a regular curriculum, or by themselves as strategies to accommodate student creativity and inventiveness.

PART II: MAKING THE UNCONVENTIONAL CONVENTIONAL.

This section contains student activities that are to be used as an introduction to PART III. These activities are geared to spur thinking in "far-out" and original patterns; they are "entryways" for the processes that follow.

PART III: THE UNCONVENTIONAL INVENTION ACTIVITIES.

Student activities that accommodate the inventive thinking and creativity processes are in this section. Accompanying each student activity page is a TEACHER DIRECTIONS page. It contains suggestions, ideas and options for introducing, using, and following up on each activity.

1

PART IV: LESSON PLANNING FOR INVENTIVE THINKING.

This section contains further suggestions for activities that will encourage inventive and creative thinking through a variety of classroom projects and instructional approaches.

PART V: UNCONVENTIONAL INVENTION PATENT.

This is a reproducible certificate which can be awarded to students who have produced inventive products.

How to use this book:

FIRST........Read PART I for an overview of creativity and the creative thinking and doing processes.

SECOND...Choose a few activities from PART II. The concept of originality and inventiveness is introduced to students here, where outlandish ideas are prized. Build up this notion of IDEA-ACCEPTANCE: thinking in original and inventive realms can be fun.

THIRD.......It is NOT necessary to use every activity in PART III. It would be advisable to select activities so that equal amounts of the six inventive thinking processes are used. (The process for each activity is stated at the top of each TEACHER DIRECTIONS page.) Accompany the activities with questions that contain the word "FUNCTION." Ask frequently, "How does it FUNCTION?" "In what ways would it cause you to FUNCTION?"

FOURTH..Award inventive thinking by issuing UNCONVEN-TIONAL INVENTION PATENT certificates which can be found in PART V. Make sure all students receive one. Award these on the basis of the best from each individual student and not on the basis of the best in the class. A "patent commit-tee" of students could create a criterion for inventiveness to help individuals iden-tify their best.

FIFTH.......Incorporate into your lesson plans some of the ideas from the 100 ideas in PART IV.

Part I:
The Nuts and Bolts of Unconventional Inventing

WHAT IS INVENTIVE THINKING?

Inventive thinking is concerned with the creation of unique products. It is the intellectual operation of one process (or a combination of several processes) which results in originality. The inventive processes used and encouraged in this book are REVERSING, DESIGNING, REDESIGNING, FINDING NEW USES, IMPROVING and INVENTING.

REVERSING means. . .   trying opposite approaches,
          such as zag before you zig,

      changing things around,

      making the negative positive
          and the positive negative,

      turning things upside down,
          outside in and inside out.

REVERSING, under certain circumstances, may be a viable solution to a problem or a way of making things work better. It is extremely useful as a device for generating ideas and gaining information about whatever is being investigated. REVERSING is a wonderful vehicle for expanding alternatives and gathering data.

DESIGNING means. . .   converging and constructing,
arranging smaller ideas to form a
larger idea,
laying out patterns,
making things fit,
mixing things for a blend,
thinking of a way to do something.

DESIGNING is the act of using what's usable. It is the placement of pieces to form a statement: the converging after the diverging.

REDESIGNING means. . . creating new patterns from existing
ones by shuffling parts,
by rearranging things,
by making modifications (like making things bigger or smaller),
or by putting things in or taking
things out.

REDESIGNING is at the heart of the inventive process because it implies that there ARE other ways of doing things! REDESIGNING requires manipulation of intellectual concepts before improvement on something it attempted.

FINDING NEW USES means. . . putting to a use other than what
was intended,
making things flexible,
thinking across categories,
looking at something in a different way,
doing something in a different way,
discovering the "aha!" in things.

FINDING NEW USES for things requires flexibility. Looking at things from many different frames of reference and from many different angles will promote and generate new ideas and will spark new insights.

IMPROVING means. . . advancing the quality of things by
    searching for,
reaching,
finding solutions through refinement,
finding better ways of doing things.

The act of **IMPROVING** things really includes problem-solving processes! It involves the asking of questions such as: "What is it I want to improve?" "Why do I want to improve it?" "What's the best way of improving it?" "How many ways are there to improve it?" "How will I know if I have improved it?" "Am I satisfied with the improvement?"

INVENTING means. . . taking provocative leaps,
thinking laterally[1], then vertically,
trying the unconventional by challenging
    accepted concepts,
visualizing what's behind and beyond
    closed doors,
making the unfamiliar familiar and
    the familiar unfamiliar,
        for building up, sorting through, and
        selecting ideas to make things work.

INVENTING is putting the processes together to form a statement of original thought. It's the visualization of how something might function and planning a way to make it function.

[1]Edward de Bono uses the words "lateral thinking" to distinguish between the "natural gift-artistic production" concept of the word CREATIVITY and the processes associated with creative thinking. The implication is that "lateral thinking" generates ideas while "vertical thinking" (logical thinking) develops them. (See *Lateral Thinking, Creativity, Step by Step,* 1973.)

HOW TO GENERATE
STUDENT INVENTIVENESS

The inventive processes described on the previous pages can be applied to a wide assortment of tasks. As the teacher encourages these six processes (REVERSING, DESIGNING, REDESIGNING, FINDING NEW IDEAS, IMPROVING, INVENTING), it is important to cultivate, as well, the processes of creative thinking. For it is by watching these that we can measure a student's inventiveness. These creative thinking processes are as follows:

FLUENCY. . . . . . . .the production of a *large number* of ideas, products or plans

FLEXIBILITY. . . . . . the production of ideas or products that show a *variety* of possibilities or realms of thought

ORIGINALITY. . . . . . the production of ideas that are *unique* or unusual

ELABORATION. . . . . the production of ideas that display *intensive detail* or enrichment

The special classroom activities described on the following pages are suggested because they will help teachers lead students toward increased creative and inventive thinking. These eight techniques described should ever be a part of classroom experience. Read them carefully, keep them in your mind, and incorporate them consistently into classroom activities within all subject areas!

BRAINSTORMING

Before quality ideas can emerge, a large base of ideas is a necessity. The method of generating ideas as a group is called BRAINSTORMING. (Osborn, 1953) Use BRAINSTORMING by following these simple rules:

1. ACCEPT EVERYTHING! Withhold criticism or evaluation of ideas. They can be censored or refined later.

2. WELCOME THE OUTLANDISH! New ideas are born only when the freedom to hatch them exists. Encourage the wild and different!

3. DON'T STOP TOO SOON! Quantity is important, because the greater the number of ideas generated, the more likely is the occurrence of the unusual.

4. YOU PARTICIPATE TOO! When students are brainstorming, the teacher should contribute as well. Your addition to the pool of ideas can demonstrate divergence and add excitement to the process.

5. BUILD and COMBINE with "OLD" IDEAS! It is valuable to brainstorm ways that existing ideas can be bettered or to gather possibilities for combining two or more ideas into a third idea.

There are all kinds of opportunities for BRAINSTORMING in the classroom. Use the technique as a means of gathering ideas for a creative writing task, as a tool for solving classroom problems, or as an introductory activity to any new topic, question or unit about to be studied.

BUILDING UP ALTERNATIVES

Exploring other ways of looking at things is critical to the growth of inventiveness. The viewing of things from different angles will promote restructuring or rearranging of information and generation of more ideas. Here are some ways to encourage the BUILDING UP of ALTERNATIVES:

1. Try some exercises using simple geometric shapes. For example, draw a square and ask students to slice the square into four equal parts, in as many different ways as they can. There are infinite ALTERNATIVES for accomplishing this task. Most students will begin with equal vertical or horizontal lines. Encourage them to try diagonal or curved lines.

This is one way to slice the square into four equal parts.

Can you think of other ways?

2. Try BUILDING UP ALTERNATIVES during classroom questioning by cuing students with "starters" such as:

"Think of different ways to..."

"List other possibilities for..."

"What else might be considered?"

"How many different ways could you tell someone...?"

"How many different uses can you think of for...?"

"In what ways might a school building be used over the summer months to serve retired people?"

BUILDING UP ALTERNATIVES (cont'd.)

3. The following checklist, called SCAMPER, (Eberle, 1971) is a mnemonic device designed to help you remember some ALTERNATIVE ways of looking at things, situations or problems. Use this with your students!

S	SUBSTITUTE	Have a thing or person act or serve in another's place.
C	COMBINE	Bring together or unite.
A	ADAPT	Adjust to suit a condition or purpose.
M	MODIFY	Alter or change the form or quality.
	MAGNIFY	Enlarge or make greater in quality or form.
	MINIFY	Make smaller, lighter, slower, less frequent.
P	PUT TO OTHER USES	Use for purposes other than the one intended.
E	ELIMINATE	Remove, omit, get rid of a quality, part or whole.
R	REARRANGE	Change order or adjust; create another layout or scheme.

4. Use ambiguities for developing or showing ALTERNATE ways of looking at things. For example, gather photographs (or magazine or newspaper pictures) for which there may be many interpretations as to what is happening. Ask students to speculate on the occurrences shown in the pictures. OR, you might take a paragraph out of a story. Read it to the class and ask students to surmise what might have occurred in the story to that point. OR show the beginning of a movie and ask students to suggest alternate endings. The important factor in this kind of an activity is to provide the group opportunity for a wide variety of interpretations and alternate approaches.

ATTRIBUTING

When one looks into the characteristics of something, more information is gathered and more ideas emerge. Attribute-listing is a simple activity that yields a payload of information.

Try it by asking students to list the properties or attributes of almost anything. Take, for example, a lamp shade and an alarm clock.

Attributes of a lamp shade	Attributes of an alarm clock
It softens and narrows light.	Gives you the time.
It projects or places light where you want it to be.	Wakes you up when you want to be awakened.
It comes in various shapes and sizes.	Comes in various styles.
It can be purchased rather easily in stores.	Can be purchased in stores easily.
It can be aesthetic and highlight room decor.	Can match room decor.
It can sit on a table.	Can be placed on a table.

Combine the attributes of a lamp shade with the attributes of an alarm clock. What might the combined attributes suggest? How about an alarm clock that places or projects light on a wall or ceiling? Suppose the light projected the time on a wall or ceiling. What benefits would this serve? Someone did combine the attributes for a brand new product that is now available in stores.

Use this activity with people, too! By looking at the attributes of selected leaders, the attributes of leadership will appear. Try it with famous scientists for finding the attributes of persons connected with discovery and invention.

ASSOCIATING

An analogy becomes an analogy when it is compared to something else! Analogies are wonderful for getting away from commonplace modes of thought. Here, the word ASSOCIATING is being used, for the word implies comparison. The associations discussed are sometimes forced, sometimes not. Forcing associations is a type of activity that deals in metaphors, because it forces thinking in broad metaphorical terms. Another thing that forced association does is generate ideas--LOTS of them!

Here are some examples of forced associations (from *Sunflowering*, Stanish, 1977):

"In what ways can warmth be seen?"

"How would you feel if you were a fallen sequoia tree?"

"Which is funnier--a triangle or a square? Why?"

The last question represents the type of analogy concept developed by the Synectics Corporation (Gordon, 1961) in which emphasis is placed on "making the strange familiar and making the familiar strange." Associations of this kind enhance the production of alternatives.

Questions that call for ASSOCIATING provide stimuli for looking at things from many different perspectives. Slide two seemingly incomparable things into a sentence structure such as:

"How is a _____ like a _____?"

"What is the same about a _____ and a _____?"

Because an open-ended question has no one "right" answer, but a multitude of answers, it is the kind to ask for generating the production of inventive ideas. REFRAIN from judging responses of this type. At a later time (and for refinement or evaluative purposes) questioning that calls for more convergent or logical response can be asked. Questions can either be expanding or restricting--make sure yours are expanding!!

GENERATING IDEAS
THROUGH RANDOM WORDS

A THINK TANK is a plastic sphere with a device that shuffles words. This "contraption," which works in conjunction with the human mind, was developed by Savo Bojicic. Here's how it works: the words appear at random through a window. The person or group makes associations between the words and the functions each word might suggest in relation to a particular problem under investigation. In his book, *Think Tank, A New Tool for the Mind* (1973,) Edward de Bono describes how the THINK TANK can promote lateral thinking. (Refer back to page 7 for an explanation of "logical thinking.")

You can easily use the THINK TANK idea in a classroom. Make a MINI THINK TANK from a shoe box. Have students fill the shoe box with a hundred or more random nouns, adjectives and verbs which they've written on small cards. (Encourage them to use dictionaries in collecting their words.)

Then, propose a problem or a task. For example: "REDESIGN THE HUMAN BODY." A student may go to the MINI THINK TANK, shake the box, and pull out four words. Suppose the words are: BRAKE, FAIRWAY, JUMP, SAPPY. Ask the student to write down the function each of these words implies.

BRAKE......A device for stopping or slowing motion.

FAIRWAY...A stretch of ground on a golf course free of obstacles for movement.

JUMP........To spring up off the ground.

SAPPY......Full of juice; juicy; sticky.

What might be suggested to the student, through association, would be a way to slow down the respiratory system during times of stress OR the possibility of designing a better way for a body to move around obstacles, etc. Not all the words of functions need to be used. This is just a way of getting students started on their thinking about a task.

GENERATING IDEAS THROUGH RANDOM WORDS does take practice! Progress will show with experience.

SYNTHESIZING

SYNTHESIS is a combining process. Fresh ideas, facts and information often come to the surface when something is placed in combination with something else. This new relationship creates a new entity!

There are very simple ways to accommodate SYNTHESIS in the classroom. When you ask students to summarize something they've completed or when you ask them to simplify an explanation, you are activating SYNTHESIS. An excellent end-of-the-school-day activity is to ask students to respond to the question, "What did I learn today?" OR "What new ideas will I take away with me today?" This question promotes SYNTHESIZING well.

Generate SYNTHESIS in your classroom by consistent use of questions of this type:

"What could you make more beautiful by making it wetter?"

"What could you make more enjoyable by making it slower?"

"What could be made more enjoyable by making it longer?"

The book, *Invitations to Speaking and Writing Creatively* (Torrance and Myers, 1965), contains many activities based on questions of this kind. These will prove to be good SYNTHESIZING experiences for your students.

VISUALIZING

In the book, *I Believe in Unicorns,* (Stanish, 1979), an activity is entitled SUPERMACHINE. The "Supermachine" illustration is a type of contraption which has a pedal device with human feet. A ball is kicked into a chamber. It appears that a process is changing the properties of the ball. The remains of the ball are transmitted to another chamber which has a door. Students are asked to visualize what occurred to the ball and what's behind the closed door.

The use of imagination to visualize and fantasize "what's behind closed doors" is still another way of stimulating ideas. This skill is extremely important for developing originality and inventiveness. It can provide glimpses into what needs to be done before synthesis can take place.

Problem-solving processes require VISUALIZING the hidden aspects of a problem. These hidden aspects of a problem must be handled before an effective solution is attained. If not, the problem becomes fuzzier. (Noller, Parnes, and Biondi, 1976); (Eberle and Stanish, 1980).

Promoting visualization can easily be accomplished by providing student activities of this type:

"Describe the sights and sounds that would be around you if you were a tomato seed inside of a tomato."

"Imagine you are traveling through the outer realms of our galaxy. Write a travel log of your impressions and feelings."

"Pretend you could miniaturize yourself and enter a typewriter. Think about all the things that could prevent the typewriter from typing."

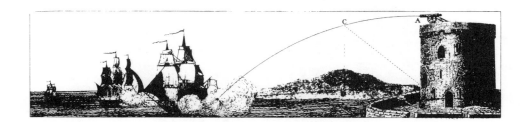

ROLE PLAYING

Assuming the characteristics of a product (or *becoming* the product) or of a person closely related to the product will often promote additional insights and start more ideas developing. Encourage students to pantomime the operation of their inventions. In PART II of this book you will find an activity called "Invent a Pick-Up-Your-Mess Machine " (Activity #6). Ask students to perform the function of each part of this invention. Doing so will demonstrate the student-inventor's concept of how the machine should work AND will suggest to the originator some improvements which might be made upon her invention.

Students can also ROLE PLAY spontaneous dialogues between an improved and an unimproved item. Use such an activity in conjunction with any of the PART III activities which focus on the inventive thinking process of IMPROVING. Additional suggestions for improving the item will occur as a pair of students in the roles of the actual unimproved and improved inventions.

Also use public interviews with student groups. Have a student assume the role of the product. Then ask questions about his/her invention such as those questions suggested in the next section, QUESTIONING FOR CLARIFICATION.

Some other ways in which students may use ROLE PLAYING to improve the quality of inventions are:

ROLE PLAY a patent official and an inventor with an invention.

ROLE PLAY consumers making positive statements about a product.

ROLE PLAY things in need of improvement. Have "consumers" suggest
means of improving the items.

ROLE PLAY the combination of totally different items. For example, combine
two newly invented student inventions to create a brand new invention.

ROLE PLAY commercials for invented products.

ROLE PLAY malfunctions of real equipment and/or malfunctions of student inventions.

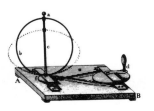

17

QUESTIONING FOR CLARIFICATION

Helping students to clarify their thinking can be a valuable teaching strategy. It avoids judging, moralizing and criticizing by the teacher and places the responsibility on students to develop and examine their own ideas.

To provide students with ready answers and solutions to the activities in THE UNCONVENTIONAL INVENTION BOOK would be a disservice to the rationale of accommodating original thinking. Many student notions will appear somewhat fuzzy and undeveloped as they seek out ways to untangle some of the paradoxes and problems associated with the activities. Assist them by using questions of this kind:

"Can you tell me how you arrived at that idea?"

"Can you give me some examples of your idea?"

"What do you mean by . . .?"

"Are you saying . . .?" (Repeat student statement.)

"What would the benefits be of this . . .?"

"Are there other possibilities here?"

"Is there another way of doing it?"

"What makes this idea workable?"

"What other ideas did you consider?" "Why did you reject the other ideas?"

"Where will this idea lead?"

"What will be the effect of this?"

"Is there anything else that can be done?"

QUESTIONING FOR CLARIFICATION (cont'd.)

"What other uses are there?"

"What other changes are possible?"

"Can it be modified?" "In what ways?"

"What changes will this idea effect?" "Are you satisfied with these changes?"

"Can you explain how this will work?"

"What might keep your idea from working well?"

"What might cause your invention to become obsolete?"

"What would happen if you combined your idea with _____'s idea?"

"Who might be the best user of your invention?"

"What hesitations or questions do you have about your idea?"

"Were there any things that happened along the way that might have taken your idea in a different direction?"

"What kind of an idea would you like to pursue next?"

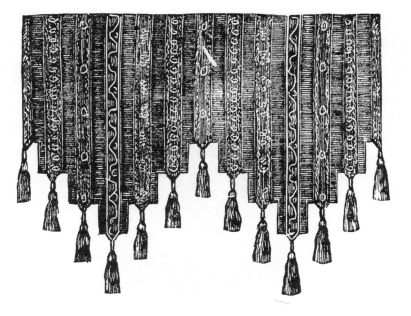

De Bono, Edward, *Lateral Thinking, Creativity Step by Step.* New York: Harper & Row, 1973.

De Bono, Edward, *Think Tank, A New Tool for the Mind.* Toronto: Think Tank Corporation, 1973.

Eberle, Bob, and Stanish, Bob, *CPS for Kids: A Resource Book for Teaching Creative Problem Solving to Children.* Buffalo: D.O.K. Publishers, 1980.

Eberle, Bob, *Scamper, Games for Imagination Development.* Buffalo: D.O.K. Publishers, 1971.

Gordon, William J.J., *Synectics.* New York: Harper & Row Publishers, 1961.

Noller, Ruth B., Parnes, Sidney J., and Biondi, Angelo M., *Creative Actionbook.* New York: Charles Scribner's Sons, 1976.

Osborn, Alex F., *Applied Imagination.* New York: Charles Scribner's Sons, 1953.

Stanish, Bob, *I Believe in Unicorns: Classroom Experiences for Activating Creative Thinking.* Carthage, IL: Good Apple, Inc., 1979.

Stanish, Bob, *Sunflowering: Thinking, Feeling, Doing Activities for Creative Expression.* Carthage, IL: Good Apple, Inc., 1977.

Torrance, E. Paul, and Myers, Robert E., *Invitations to Speaking and Writing Creatively.* Lexington, MA: Ginn and Co., 1965.

Torrance, E. Paul, *Guiding Creative Talent.* Englewood Cliffs, N J : Prentice-Hall, 1962.

BIBLIOGRAPHY

Barron, Frank, *Creativity and Personal Freedom.* New York: Van Nostrand Reinhold, 1968.

Bingham, Alma, *Improving Children's Facility in Problem Solving.* New York: Bureau of Publications, Teachers College, Columbia University, 1963.

Biondi, Angelo M., ed., *Have an Affair with Your Mind.* Great Neck, NY: Creative Synergetic Association, 1974.

Biondi, Angelo M., ed., *The Creative Process.* Buffalo: D.O.K. Publishers, 1973.

Brown, George I., *Human Teaching for Human Learning.* San Francisco: Esalen Institute, 1971.

Bruner, Jerome, *On Knowing.* New Haven, CT: Harvard University Press, 1962.

Davis, Gary, *Psychology of Problem Solving: Theory and Practice.* New York: Basic Books, 1973.

De Bono, Edward, *Lateral Thinking, Creativity Step by Step.* New York: Harper & Row, 1973.

De Bono, Edward, *Think Tank, A New Tool for the Mind.* Toronto: Think Tank Corporation, 1973.

Eberle, Bob, and Stanish, Bob, *CPS for Kids: A Resource Book for Teaching Creative Problem Solving to Children.* Buffalo: D.O.K. Publishers, 1980.

Eberle, Bob, *Scamper, Games for Imagination Development.* Buffalo: D.O.K. Publishers, 1971.

Feldhusen, J.F., and Treffinger, D.J., *Teaching Creative Thinking and Problem Solving.* Dubuque: Kendall-Hunt, 1977.

Getzels, J.W., and Jackson, P.W., *Creativity and Intelligence.* New York: Wiley, 1962.

Gordon, William J.J., *Synectics.* New York: Harper & Row Publishers, 1961.

Gowen, John Curtis, *Development of the Creative Individual.* San Diego: Knapp Publishers, 1972.

Gowen, John C., *Trance, Art, and Creativity.* Buffalo: The Creative Education Foundation, 1975.

Guilford, J.P., *The Nature of Human Intelligence.* New York: McGraw-Hill, 1967.

Hudgins, Bryce B., *Problem Solving in the Classroom.* New York: Macmillan, 1966.

Koberg, Don, and Bagnall, Jim, *The Universal Traveler.* Los Altos, CA: William Kaufman, Inc., 1972.

MacKinnon, Donald W., *In Search of Human Effectiveness, Identifying and Developing Creativity.* Buffalo: The Creative Education Foundation, 1978.

McKim, Robert H., *Experiences in Visual Thinking.* Belmont, CA: Brooks/Cole Publishing Company, 1972.

Meeker, Mary Nacol, *The Structure of Intellect: Its Interpretations and Uses.* Columbus, OH: Charles E. Merrill Publishing Company, 1969.

Noller, Ruth B., *Scratching the Surface of Creative Problem Solving, A Bird's Eye View of CPS.* Buffalo: D.O.K. Publishers, 1977.

Noller, Ruth B., Parnes, Sidney J., and Biondi, Angelo M., *Creative Actionbook.* New York: Charles Scribner's Sons, 1976.

Noller, Ruth B., Treffinger, Donald J., and Houseman, Elwood D., *It's a Gas to be Gifted, or CPS for the Gifted and Talented.* Buffalo: D.O.K. Publishers, 1979.

Osborn, Alex F., *Applied Imagination.* New York: Charles Scribner's Sons, 1953.

Parnes, Sidney J., *Aha, Insights into Creative Behavior.* Buffalo: D.O.K. Publishers, 1975.

Parnes, Sidney J., Noller, Ruth B., and Biondi, Angelo M., *Guide to Creative Action.* New York: Charles Scribner's Sons, 1976.

Renzulli, Joseph S., *New Dimensions in Creativity,* Volumes Mark 1, Mark 2, and Mark 3. New York: Harper & Row Publishers, 1973.

BIBLIOGRAPHY (cont'd.)

Stanish, Bob, *I Believe in Unicorns: Classroom Experiences for Activating Creative Thinking.* Carthage, IL: Good Apple, Inc., 1979.

Stanish, Bob, *Sunflowering: Thinking, Feeling, Doing Activities for Creative Expression.* Carthage, IL: Good Apple, Inc., 1977.

Torrance, E. Paul, *Guiding Creative Talent.* Englewood Cliffs, NJ: Prentice-Hall, 1962.

Torrance, E. Paul, *Rewarding Creative Behavior.* Englewood Cliffs, NJ: Prentice-Hall, 1965.

Torrance, E. Paul, *The Search for Satori and Creativity.* Buffalo: The Creative Education Foundation, 1979.

Torrance, E. Paul, and Myers, Robert E., *Creative Learning and Teaching.* New York: Harper & Row, 1970.

Vincent, William S., *Indicators of Quality*, "Signs of Good Teaching." Institute of Administrative Research, Teachers College, New York: Columbia University, 1969.

Weinstein, G., and Fantini, Mario, *Toward Humanistic Education.* New York: Praeger, 1970.

Williams, Frank E., *Classroom Ideas for Encouraging Thinking and Feeling.* Buffalo, NY: D.O.K. Publishers, Inc., 1970.

Williams, Margery, *The Velveteen Rabbit.* Garden City, NY: Doubleday and Company, Inc., 1968.

Part II:
Making the Unconventional Conventional

PART II, "MAKING THE UNCONVENTIONAL CONVENTIONAL," is for causing students, in a fun-sort-of-way, to acclimate themselves to thinking in unique and "far-out" patterns. Ideas become limited when thinking is expected in logical staircase patterns. At a later time and after the generation of many ideas, logical thinking and criterion selection for the most workable ideas can be made. But for now, accustom students to thinking "far-out" by selecting a few activities from this section as a beginning point for introducing THE UNCONVENTIONAL INVENTION BOOK.

In PART III, there are teacher suggestions and directions for using THE UNCONVENTIONAL INVENTION ACTIVITIES. However, for this Part, PART II, there are not. There is a reason for this. It is important that students discover for themselves the richness in thought that unconventional thinking can stimulate.

Here are a few tactics to keep in mind while using these PART II activities:

1. Allow time for completion and total group sharing.

2. Have fun with the activities. Don't grade them, but do display them.

3. Don't try to use all of the activities in PART II. Select several for the entire class or divide the activities among the total class.

4. Don't be critical with student responses or drawings. Find something of value in each one and encourage students with praise whenever possible.

MAKING THE UNCONVENTIONAL CONVENTIONAL
Activity No. 1

1. Take a look at this invention. Describe what it's for and how it might work.

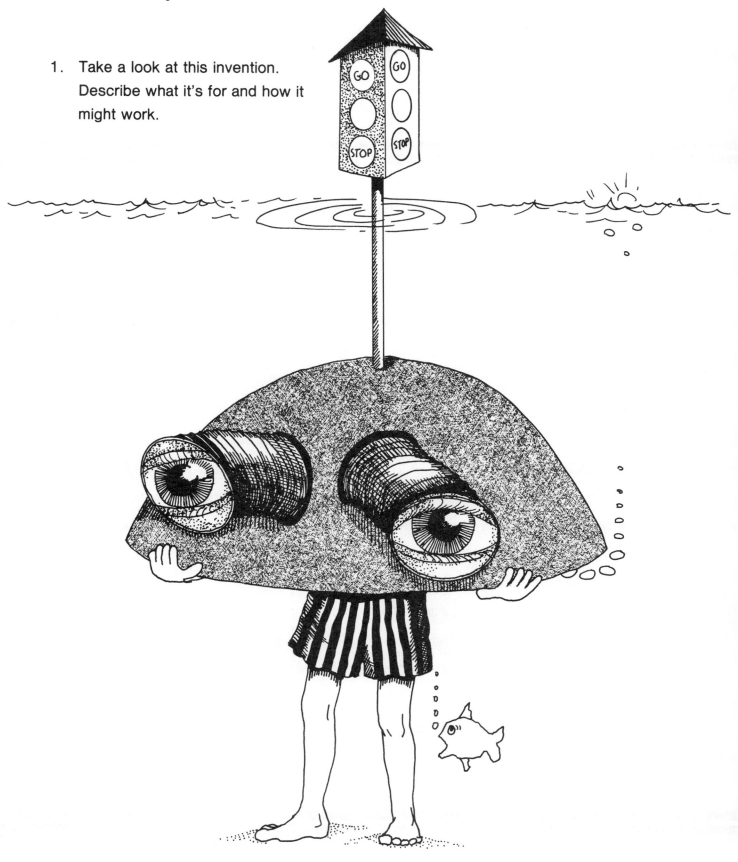

2. After describing the invention, give it a name.

_____.

3. Write a "Want Ad" description of an available job for the operator of this invention. Be sure to give the personal qualifications for the job.

*** WANT ADS ***

WANTED:

MAKING THE UNCONVENTIONAL CONVENTIONAL
Activity No. 2

1. Take a look at this vehicle and describe its advantages for dogs and dog owners.

    For dogs: _____

    _____

    _____

    _____

    For dog owners: _____

    _____

    _____

    _____

2. Give this vehicle-invention a name.

    _____

3. Now it's your turn. Put this elephant on a vehicle.

4. Give your elephant-vehicle a name.

_____

5. List some advantages of your invention for big elephants.

_____

_____

MAKING THE UNCONVENTIONAL CONVENTIONAL
Activity No. 3

There are many different kinds of robots
that do different kinds of things.

1. Think of some things you could
   program this robot to do. Write
   them here.

_____

_____

_____

_____

_____

_____

_____

_____

_____

2. Now imagine that after programming your robot, it got short-circuited and did unusual things in a supermarket.

    Write a newspaper headline and article about the mishap.

MAKING THE UNCONVENTIONAL CONVENTIONAL
Activity No. 4

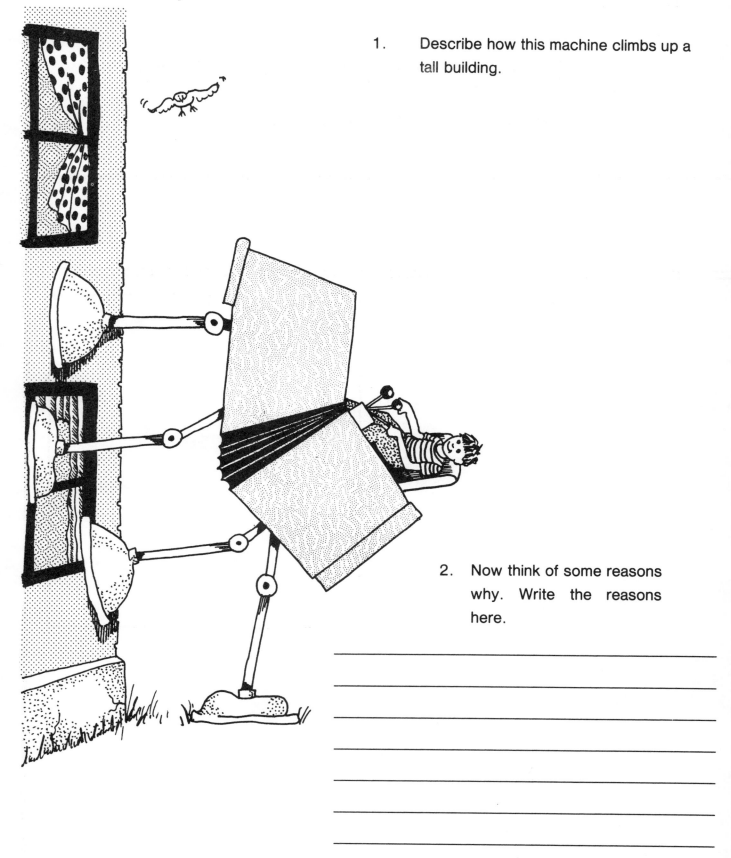

1. Describe how this machine climbs up a tall building.

2. Now think of some reasons why. Write the reasons here.

_____

_____

_____

_____

_____

_____

_____

_____

MAKING THE UNCONVENTIONAL CONVENTIONAL
Activity No. 4, continued

3. Finish the drawing below of "the economy two-plunger model for home use."

4. Write a 30-second radio commercial for the two-plunger model.

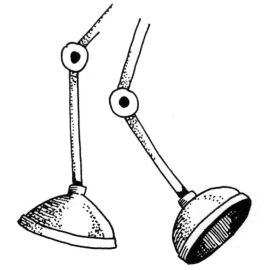

MAKING THE UNCONVENTIONAL CONVENTIONAL
Activity No. 5

1. Name it.

_____

_____

_____

_____

2. Describe it.

_____

_____

_____

_____

_____

_____

_____

_____

MAKING THE UNCONVENTIONAL CONVENTIONAL
Activity No. 5, CONTINUED

3. On this billboard, design and write a rhyming jingle about litter and the invention you named.

MAKING THE UNCONVENTIONAL CONVENTIONAL
Activity No. 6

1. Can you invent a "pick-up-your-mess" machine? A portion of it has already been done. Finish the invention.

2. Describe how it works.

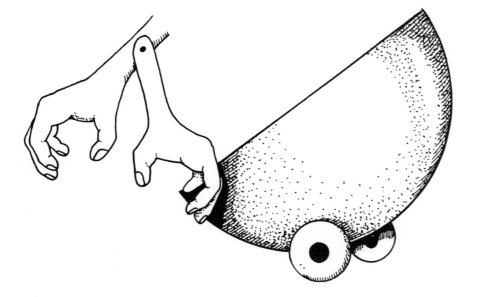

3. Other than "messes," what could you use the machine for? (How about in the garden or the yard or on fairgrounds?)

    _____

    _____

    _____

    _____

    _____

    _____

    _____

    _____

    _____

4. Select your favorite use from above and rename the machine accordingly.

    _____

    _____

MAKING THE UNCONVENTIONAL CONVENTIONAL
Activity No. 7

1.   What do these strange creatures have in common?

2.   What do you suppose is the function of this strange invention?

3.   Name the strange invention.

4.   Create some more strange creatures that could be products of the strange invention.

MAKING THE UNCONVENTIONAL CONVENTIONAL
Activity No. 8

1. Bill feels he would receive more concert dates if he added another section or so to his band (such as strings and percussion).

    List some possibilities here for things he could add.

    _____

    _____

    _____

    _____

    _____

Now look at the next page.

2. Draw some of your ideas. Make sure they can be reached by Bill's other invention.

Activity No. 9

The Gooditch Company would like a blimp like the other company's.

This is one idea.

1. Write some other blimp ideas here.

_____

_____

_____

_____

_____

_____

_____

GOODITCH

2. Draw your best blimp idea from the last page around the name Gooditch. Add your own clouds.

MAKING THE UNCONVENTIONAL CONVENTIONAL
Activity No. 10

Mr. Brown developed giant hybrid corn which became very profitable for him.

He needs help in figuring out what to do with the giant leftover cobs.

1. Any suggestions?

_____

_____

_____

_____

_____

_____

_____

_____

_____

2. Take one of your favorite ideas and write a description of it or draw the idea in and around this giant corncob.

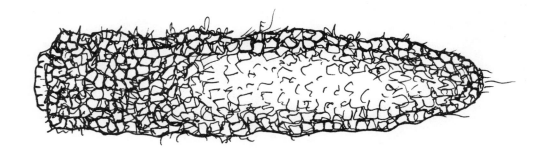

MAKING THE UNCONVENTIONAL CONVENTIONAL
Activity No. 11

1. What's the function of this? _____

_____

_____

_____

_____

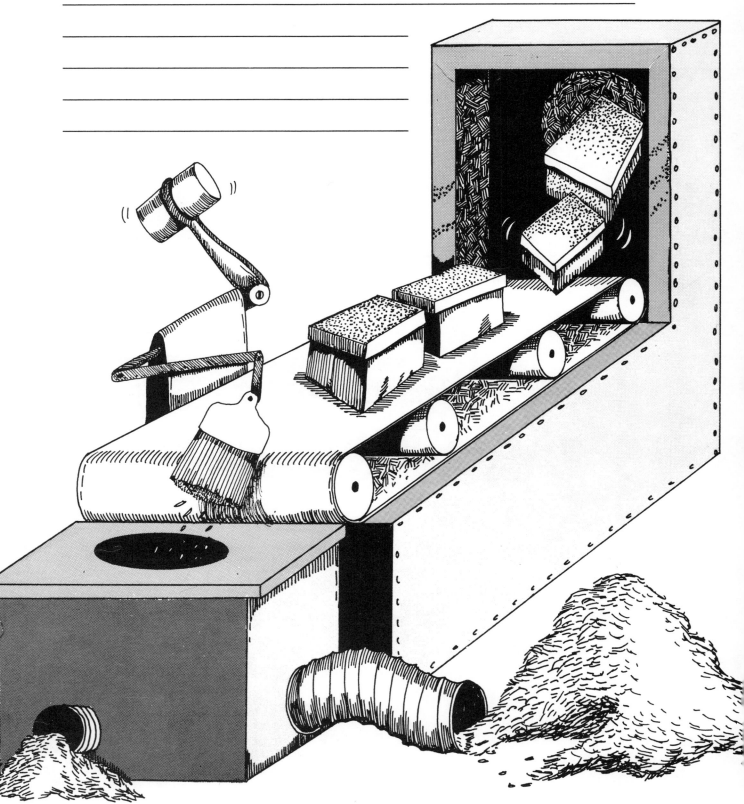

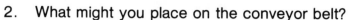

2. What might you place on the conveyor belt?

_____

_____

_____

_____

_____

_____

_____

_____

_____

_____

_____

_____

_____

MAKING THE UNCONVENTIONAL CONVENTIONAL
Activity No. 12

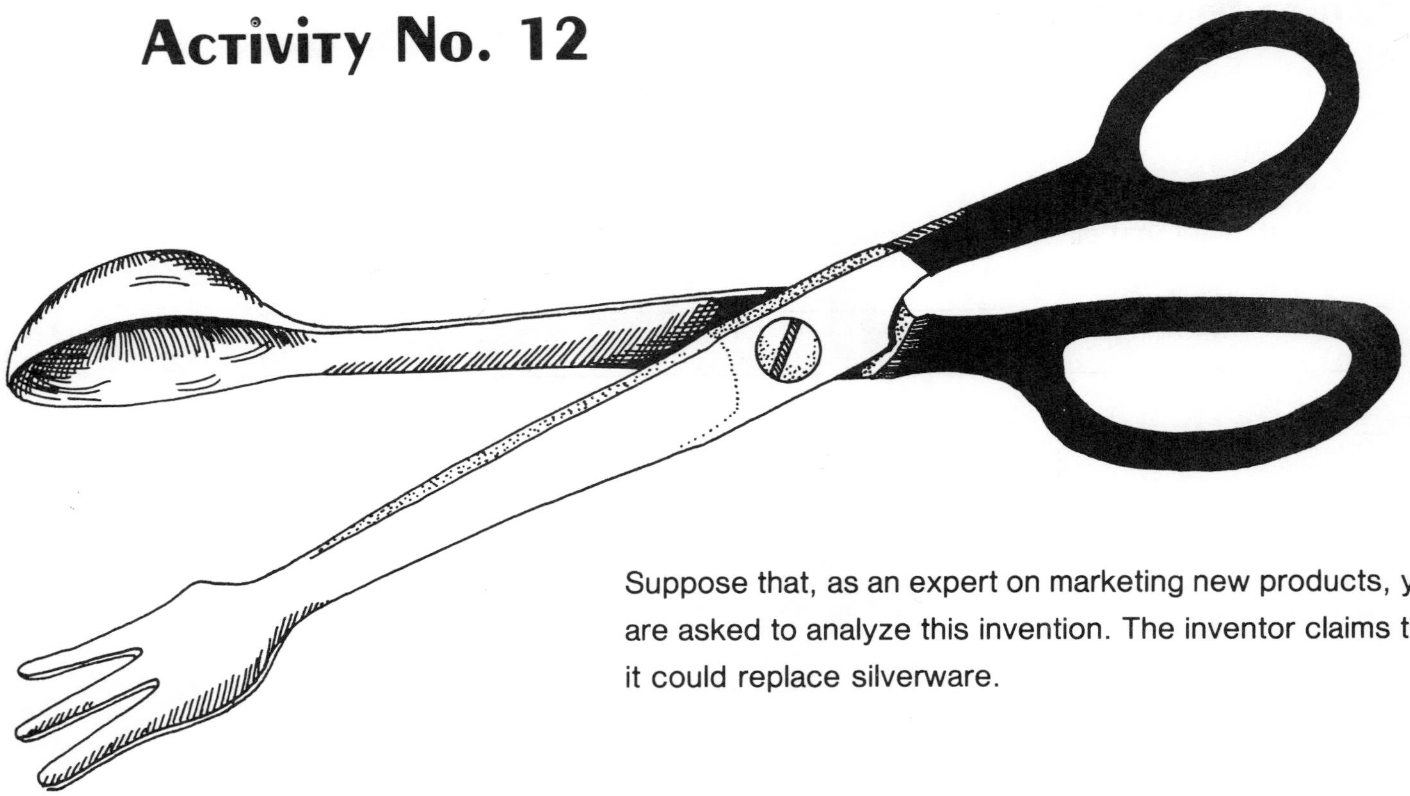

Suppose that, as an expert on marketing new products, you are asked to analyze this invention. The inventor claims that it could replace silverware.

1. List the invention's functions as you perceive them.

_____

_____

_____

_____

_____

_____

_____

_____

_____

_____

2. List ways the invention could malfunction.

_____

_____

_____

_____

_____

_____

_____

3. Comparing the functions with the possible malfunctions, what would be your recommendation? Should the inventor market it or forget it? Give some reasons for your decision.

_____

_____

_____

_____

_____

_____

_____

_____

_____

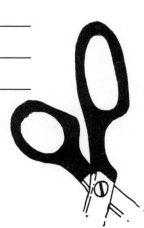

PART III:
THE UNCONVENTIONAL
INVENTION ACTIVITIES

A FEW TEACHING TIPS

for using the

UNCONVENTIONAL INVENTION Activities:

1. DON'T JUDGE. AVOID SAYING, "THIS WOULD NOT WORK BECAUSE. . ."

2. ENCOURAGE STUDENTS TO CHALLENGE ASSUMPTIONS.

3. IN LOOKING AT STUDENT PRODUCTS, SEPARATE FUNCTIONS FROM ORNAMENTATION.

4. DON'T LIMIT STUDENT IDEAS BECAUSE OF INABILITIES TO EXPRESS THEM.

5. LOOK FOR FUNCTIONS THAT UNDERLIE A PARTICULAR DRAWING. SEPARATE THE ILLUSTRATION FROM THE INTENT. THE IDEA BEHIND THE INTENT IS THE MOST IMPORTANT.

6. QUESTION TO FIND REASONS, TO CLARIFY, TO GENERATE OTHER ALTERNATIVES AND TO STIMULATE THINKING.

7. MAKE THE CLASSROOM CLIMATE "OKAY" FOR THINKING AND BEING UNCONVENTIONAL.

BUG CRUNCHERS, SPAGHETTI STRETCHERS AND OTHER THINGS:

INVENTIVE THINKING PROCESS: Reversing

WARMING-UP:

1. Tell students that sometimes a wild and funny idea can lead to something valuable. All ideas are valuable and sometimes,with a little "taming down," an idea can be very practical even if it started out as something sort of crazy.

2. Indicate that the activity today will encourage some pretty funny results but that the results could lead to some very interesting possibilities.

IDEAS FOR THE DRAWING BOARD:

1. Read the directions on the student activity page as your students read along with you. Instruct them to fold their papers along the dotted line so that the WHAT? column is facing them.

2. Ask them to write nouns (but not the names of people or places). They are not to unfold their papers until they have completed the listing of nouns.

3. Have them unfold their papers and tell them that not every combination will work, but what they are looking for is at least one idea that could be described as an invention. Encourage them to be outlandish.

4. When they name the inventions in the last column, the names should have an -ER suffix.

5. Encourage students to select the idea that most appeals to them and describe it on the activity page. Share student ideas by asking them to explain their inventions to the class.

INVENTION FOLLOW-UPS:

1. Encourage students to suggest an idea on their list, which, if tamed down could be workable and practical as an invention. Have them suggest what kinds of improvements would be necessary.

2. Try the same process with word phrases for creating interesting picturesque patterns of language. Do this by writing WHO PHRASES, WHAT PHRASES, WHEN PHRASES, as the headings for the three columns.

BUG CRUNCHERS,
SPAGHETTI STRETCHERS and other things!

Reversing the position of words can lead to invention ideas. For example, reverse WAXING FLOORS and we have a FLOOR WAXER. But a FLOOR WAXER has already been invented. So let's go for some WILD INVENTION IDEAS.

Fold your paper on the dotted line and under WHAT? write some nouns that are not names of people or places. After completing the noun list, unfold your paper and complete the invention idea. Some combinations will NOT WORK, but you should have a couple of ideas that are workable. Take your best idea and write a description of it as an invention.

"ING" WORDS	+	WHAT?	=	THE INVENTION
1. CRUNCHING	:	BUGS	:	A BUG CRUNCHER
2. STRETCHING	:	_____	:	_____
3. SQUASHING	:	_____	:	_____
4. MIXING	:	_____	:	_____
5. CATCHING	:	_____	:	_____
6. SPREADING	:	_____	:	_____
7. POLISHING	:	_____	:	_____
8. WASHING	:	_____	:	_____

DESCRIBE YOUR BEST INVENTION.

DRESS SOME FRIENDLY ALIENS:

INVENTIVE THINKING PROCESS: Designing

WARMING-UP:

1. Suggest to students that they think of clothes that are designed for comfort. "How about clothes you wear that are designed for style?" "Which is more important, comfort or style?"

2. Ask, "If you could redesign any item of clothing for improvement, what would you like to REDESIGN?"

IDEAS FOR THE DRAWING BOARD:

1. Propose these ideas to students when you hand out this activity:

   "If you had to live in a space suit, what kinds of conveniences would you like to have in your space suit?"

   "Suppose you could take only those things of a personal nature that would fit into a shoe box on a long journey through space. What things would you take?"

   "Suppose you had an opportunity to introduce some things found on earth to some aliens from another planet. Think of some things that would make use of each of the human senses. What would you choose?"

   "Think again about how form is related to function. Our clothes are designed according to the way we are built. Aliens may not be built like us. Finish the drawing by building aliens any way you would like, then design some space suits for them. Keep in mind some ideas from the other three questions above."

2. Share and show off the designs.

INVENTION FOLLOW-UPS:

1. Have someone involved in the clothing retail business talk to your class about clothing styles and supply and demand.

2. Study the development of clothing styles over the centuries within a single culture. Look up pictures showing styles of clothing in the early Middle Ages in England, in Elizabethan England, in Victorian England and in present-day England. Note the changes.

3. Encourage students to speculate what clothing styles will be like in the year 2050? Have them explain their reasoning.

"Ideas do not always have to be useful. Ideas can be inventions or they can solve problems or they can help people --or they can simply be fun. The mind is probably the least used source of enjoyment."

Edward de Bono from **Think Tank.**

DRESS SOME FRIENDLY ALIENS

DESIGN SOME SPACE SUITS FOR A COUPLE OF FRIENDLY ALIENS.

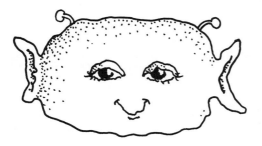

HAPPY CUPS:

INVENTIVE THINKING PROCESS: Redesigning

WARMING-UP:

1. Ask how many students have black telephones in their homes. Have students describe the styles and colors of their home telephones. Indicate that, at one time, almost everybody had the same style and color of telephone. Ask them to explain why there are so many different styles of telephones today.

2. Ask, "Other than improvements in a product, what might be some reasons why a company might redesign something differently?"

IDEAS FOR THE DRAWING BOARD:

1. Let students imagine that they are toy manufacturers. Ask, "How might you make a stuffed animal most attractive to a six-year-old?"

2. Ask students to suggest other things manufactured for children that could be redesigned for attractiveness.

3. Ask how a drinking cup might be redesigned to encourage young children to drink their milk or orange juice.

4. Distribute the activity. Encourage students to sketch several ideas on scratch paper first.

INVENTION FOLLOW-UPS:

1. Have a class discussion on how things are "packaged." Ask, "Does attractiveness make a product better? In what ways, yes? In what ways, no?"

2. Make arrangements for a consumer expert to talk to your class about consumer products and packaging.

3. Discuss the role of advertising in marketing products.

4. Have students write a commercial ad for one of their KID-APPEAL DRINKING CUPS.

5. Check with an art teacher about actually making KID-APPEAL DRINKING CUPS with your class.

HAPPY CUPS

REDESIGN A DRINKING CUP SO
THAT IT HAS **KID APPEAL**.

DO ANOTHER ONE.

UNHANG A COAT HANGER:

INVENTIVE THINKING PROCESS: Finding New Uses

WARMING-UP:

1. Ask students to describe wire sculptures.

2. Encourage students to think about where an artist might get ideas for creating wire sculptures.

3. Display a paper clip and have students guess the length of the wire. Unravel the paper clip and determine its length. Ask students, "If you had to determine different uses for a paper clip, would it be easier to think of it as a piece of wire or as a paper clip?"

4. Suggest to students that sometimes when we are looking for different uses for something, it might be helpful to view it from many different frames of reference and many different angles.

IDEAS FOR THE DRAWING BOARD:

1. Tell students that to do this activity it is important to think across categories. To think across categories, it helps to imagine looking at something upside down or sideways or inside out or by stretching something into a new shape.

2. Provide students with activity sheets and have them list different uses for a coat hanger. Encourage them to "mentally" twist the hanger in their minds. Twisted shapes might suggest to students new or different uses.

3. Upon completion, count ideas to see who had the greatest variety and quantity of responses. Those ideas that might suggest the same concept of use, for example, stir paint, stir soup, stir hot chocolate, stir oatmeal, etc., should be counted as a single use.

INVENTION FOLLOW-UPS:

1. Encourage students to select one of their ideas calling for construction and do it. Select a special day and call it THE UNHANGER DAY. Have students bring in their UNHANGERS for display.

2. Determine originality in your class by citing student ideas that were one of a kind (that is, no one else thought of the same idea).

3. Have students write a short story about a coat hanger that held a famous coat. Encourage students to research an actual event. Discuss the value of historical fiction in literature and history.

UNHANG A COAT HANGER

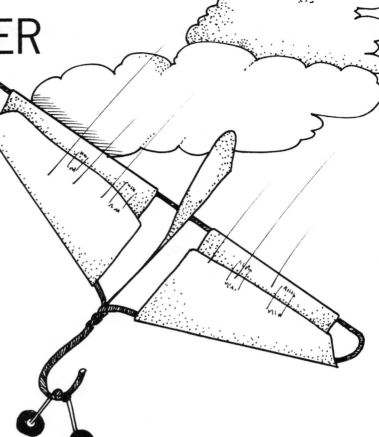

HOW MANY DIFFERENT USES FOR
A COAT HANGER?

TWIST,

BEND,

RESHAPE,

OR

JUST LEAVE ALONE.

LIST THE USES HERE.

_____

_____

_____

_____

_____

_____

_____

_____

_____

_____

_____

_____

HOW MANY DIFFERENT USES? _____

SPECIAL DELIVERY:

INVENTIVE THINKING PROCESS: Improving

WARMING-UP:

1. Ask students to describe the good things about and conveniences of an outside official government mailbox.

2. Challenge students to cite some disadvantages. Examples: At times it is awkward to deposit letters from a car. It's hard to get to in heavy traffic. Only certain size packages and envelopes will fit. There is usually only one opening and the opening might be on the street side — could create a dangerous situation for a pedestrian with letters to mail.

3. Suggest that students speculate as to why government mailboxes are shaped like they are. Would other shapes work? Would they have suggestions for better-shaped mailboxes?

IDEAS FOR THE DRAWING BOARD:

1. Suggest to students that improvements can be made on outside mail drops. Encourage them to think about mailboxes with different purposes, shapes and sizes.

2. Have students write their suggested improvements on the activity page. Allow 15 minutes. If more space is needed, encourage the continuation of ideas on the back of their activity sheets.

3. In describing their three best improvements, have students keep in mind conveniences for both postal personnel and the general public.

INVENTION FOLLOW-UPS:

1. Ask the local postmaster to talk to your class about the role of postal service. Ask the postmaster about "incentive" awards given to employees for suggestions of ways to save time and money within the agency.

2. Challenge students to list human-made products that CANNOT be improved.

3. Discuss why RETHINKING is necessary to the IMPROVEMENT of things.

4. Have a small committee of students construct a model of an "improved" mail drop.

"I invent nothing; I rediscover."

Rodin

List ways to improve a government mail drop.

_____

_____

_____

_____

_____

_____

_____

OUT OF TOWN

_____

_____

_____

_____

_____

_____

_____

_____

_____

_____

Check ✓ your 3 best improvements and describe how they would improve mailing letters and packages.

AID A GATOR (OR GATOR-AID):

INVENTIVE THINKING PROCESS: Inventing

Note: Before beginning this activity, bring a cookbook to class.

WARMING-UP:

1. Ask for a show of hands as to how many students believe that inventing should be or is applied to cooking.

2. Indicate that the art of Chinese cooking is the result of invention and innovation with edible foods due to the great famines in their history, that the people's energies were applied to whatever was available and over the course of centuries their perfection of food became famous.

3. Have students list "family recipes" that have been handed down to each generation within their families. Ask why each family recipe is special.

IDEAS FOR THE DRAWING BOARD:

1. Inform students that the great chefs of Europe are famous for their abilities to create and invent courses and items for their meals.

2. Read, at random, recipes from a cookbook. Emphasize the measurements called for in each recipe you select.

3. Encourage students to imagine what would be in a SWAMPBURGER. Most nationality foods consist of those items native to their respective regions. Have students list things that might be found in a swamp.

4. Do the activity and provide adequate time for sharing - the ideas, that is, not the SWAMPBURGERS.

INVENTION FOLLOW-UPS:

1. Ask students to compare the probable steps in inventing a machine with the probable steps in inventing a new recipe. In what ways are the steps similar?

2. Encourage a student to volunteer, in behalf of the class, to write the White House and request a State Dinner Menu. Upon receipt of the menu, examine it to see how the selections relate to the nationality of the invited guest.

3. Encourage students to "invent" a new cookie or a cheese spread, etc. Invite them to bring samples of it to school. Also encourage them to seek consultation with their mothers before the invention process gets too involved!

Aid a Gator (or Gator-Aid)

Improve the mood of an angry gator by inventing a swampburger to feed him.

List the ingredients.

Cooking instructions: (How should it be cooked? How long? etc.)

Serving suggestions: (What gets added after cooking? etc.)

Aid a Gator (or Gator-Aid)

CAR WASH:

INVENTIVE THINKING PROCESS: Reversing

WARMING-UP:

1. Ask students to suppose everyone in the world were left-handed. "What kinds of changes would you expect to see in the products we buy?"

2. Ask students, "What would happen to a musical composition if the notes were played from the last stanza to the first? Would there still be a melody?" Encourage a student to try it.

3. Ask students, "In what kinds of situations might reversing an approach to a problem be effective?"

IDEAS FOR THE DRAWING BOARD:

1. Distribute the activity.

2. Tell students to suppose that a city government was concerned about having clean downtown streets and someone suggested buying street cleaning vehicles. Suppose you REVERSED the idea and said, "How about downtown streets cleaning vehicles?"

3. Ask them to list some advantages for the scheme before the next meeting.

4. Upon completion of the written activity, have two or three students combine their items for a single listing of advantages. Formulate a group of seven students to role play city commissioners. Have a student with the combined ideas role play the presentation of the idea to the commissioners.

INVENTION FOLLOW-UPS:

1. In what way might "instant replay" be valuable to things other than televised football? How about surgical procedures? How about airplane assembly lines? Can you think of other situations in which going back and reviewing how something was done might be valuable?

2. Think of ways you could justify the statement "Backwards is sometimes forward."

3. Think about reversing some of your routines. What could you reverse in your own life?

4. Leonardo da Vinci wrote his observation and study notes backwards. Why do you suppose he did that? How was he able to refer back to them? (mirror)

Car Wash

Reverse vehicles cleaning streets

to

A street cleaning vehicle.

List the advantages.

_____

_____

_____

_____

_____

_____

_____

_____

_____

_____

_____

_____

_____

_____

Check ✓ the 3 best advantages.

INVENTIVE THINKING PROCESS: Designing

WARMING-UP:

1. Encourage students to look around the room and list things that appear to be in patterns. Look at pattern designs on blouses, shirts, etc.

2. Tell students that the world consists of patterns and designs. Some are natural (such as the structure of plant blossoms and leaf structures). Some are man-made (such as highway cloverleafs and brick decorations on houses).

3. Indicate that often a man-made design is an expression of a message. If possible, obtain a photograph of Robert Indiana's famous painting, *Love*. The placement of letters in *Love* and the intense colors make it an interesting and exciting design.

IDEAS FOR THE DRAWING BOARD:

1. Draw attention to the design on the activity page and ask students:

   "What name is in the design?" "What would happen if Tom Smith would have used the letter S to begin with and used only 9 letters on each line and extended the quilt vertically to 8 squares?" (Tom's name would also appear vertically, as well as horizontally.)

2. Inform students that creating a design takes thought. Encourage them to experiment with ideas before trying the activity sheet.

3. Have students use colored magic markers if available.

INVENTION FOLLOW-UPS:

1. Try this technique as a class project. Use butcher paper large enough to accommodate all classroom names plus messages of class or school pride.

2. Demonstrate "illusion" by making available this well-known perceptual message. To read it, look at the white spaces. If trouble seeing it still exists, try marking a horizontal line above the top and bottom borders.

NAME QUILTS

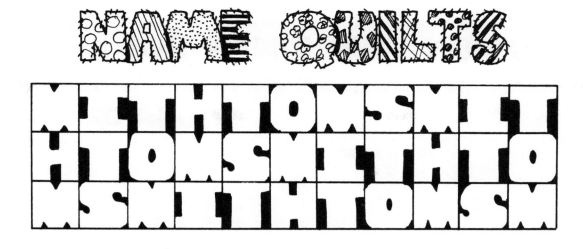

Design your name in such a way as to form a large quilt-like pattern.

REDESIGN THE HUMAN BODY:

INVENTIVE THINKING PROCESS: Redesigning

WARMING-UP:

1. Considering the strike zone in baseball (between shoulder level and knee level), where would the shoulders and arms be best located on the human body to improve batting averages? (answer: hips or ribs)

2. Discuss what possible changes would occur in typewriters, pianos, guitars, and other machines and instruments if we had seven fingers on each hand.

3. What kinds of changes in our bodies would we need to fly alongside of seagulls? How about whales?

IDEAS FOR THE DRAWING BOARD:

1. Ask students to think of things they would like to do better and things that other species of life can do that they can't do.

2. Ask, "What chemistry within the human body would you change or redesign to eliminate certain diseases? What diseases would this eliminate?"

3 Ask, "How would you redesign the human body to ensure a longer life?"

4. Do the activity sheet which follows.

INVENTION FOLLOW-UPS:

1. Ask a medical student, a doctor, a nurse or a medical scientist to talk to your class about recent advances in medical technology and how these advances are prolonging life.

2. Encourage a few students to form an interview team and interview an engineer and a surgeon. Have them compare what they do and how they approach problems in their respective fields. Afterwards, have the interview team cite the ways engineering is like medicine.

3. Encourage students to research the changes in human bodies. Encourage investigation into the size of armor worn by knights during the Middle Ages; compare the height of professional basketball centers 30 years ago with today's stars in the NBA; study scientists' conceptions of early man.

4. Study the improvement of track and field records over the years, especially in women's athletics.

"The acquisition of any knowledge is always of use to the intellect, because it may drive out useless things and preserve the good. For nothing can be loved or hated unless it is first understood."

Leonardo da Vinci

Redesign the Human Body

List the advantages of your redesign.

_____

_____

_____

_____

_____

_____

_____

_____

_____

VEGETABLES AND THINGS:

INVENTIVE THINKING PROCESS: Finding New Uses

WARMING-UP:

1. Our imaginations are great for finding new uses for almost anything. Ask students to look in their desks or pockets or purses and find objects whose designs might remind them of something else.

2. Discuss with students how the design of one thing might cause one to think of something else that has a totally different function.

IDEAS FOR THE DRAWING BOARD:

1. Distribute the student activity sheets. Although it isn't necessary, you might want to identify the vegetables on the activity sheet. They are not illustrated in accurate proportion to each other. The vegetables are a beet, a half-slice of green pepper, a squash, peas in a pod and the large oval is a tomato.

2. Also have available for students paper on which they can build a collage. It is not necessary for them to use every vegetable, but do encourage students to add whatever lines or sketches are necessary to clarify their ideas.

3. Have students jot down some ideas first about what some of the vegetable designs bring to mind. Encourage them, if possible, to combine some of the ideas into a new idea.

4. Encourage students to write a description of the function or functions of their creations. What would it be used for? What are the benefits?

5. Provide plenty of time for students to explain their creations to you and the class.

INVENTION FOLLOW-UPS:

1. Taking ideas from nature isn't new. Have students imagine what kinds of ideas engineers might gain from studying the structure of spider webs. This has actually been done with improving suspension bridges.

2. Encourage students to do reseach on how scientists have to visualize what they can't see in order to generalize functions, explanations, and theories. Start with scientists who have made contributions to our understanding of the universe.

3. For fun, try visualization of new uses for other vegetables. Draw the inside of a vegetable without slicing it.

Vegetables & Things

Cut out these vegetables and assemble a collage of something with an imaginary function. Add lines or sketches as you desire to create a space vehicle for the twenty-second century, or a new light fixture design, or anything!

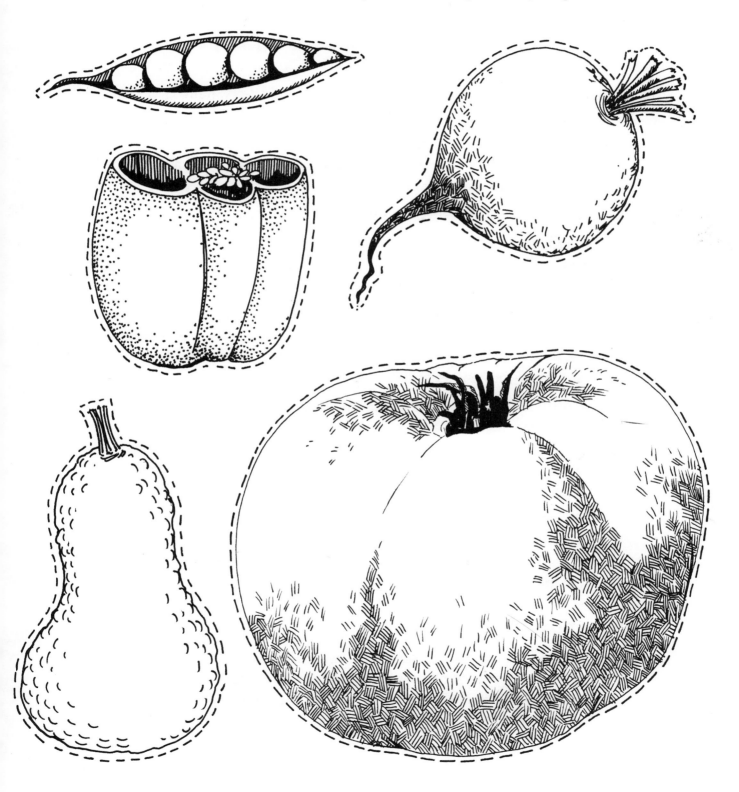

FORCE-FITTING FUNCTIONS:

INVENTIVE THINKING PROCESS: Improving

WARMING-UP:

1. Discuss with students the word "function." Indicate that almost everything in the world has a function and that many things have multi-functions.

2. When we attempt to improve or create or change something we're basically thinking about the "function" of something.

3. Suggest to students that words are functions, too. Sometimes when we think of word functions and apply them to something we want to improve or change, we can generate some helpful ideas.

IDEAS FOR THE DRAWING BOARD:

1. Ask students to carefully look over the words listed on the activity sheets. If they are not sure as to their meanings, they can look the words up in a dictionary or simply not use them.

2. Have students select three words from the list and write them on the dotted lines of the activity sheet. Next to each word, they are to write what the word's function or definition is. There may be several functions for each word, but one is all that's necessary.

3. Upon selecting the words and listing their functions, have students fit the word functions into the concept of a grocery cart. For example, the word "combine" has a word function of "joining together" which might suggest two carts with a magnetic clasp for bulk shopping. Another example might include the word "bloat" with a function of "to swell-up or puff-up." This word function might suggest inflatable grocery carts.

4. Encourage students to combine all three word functions to improve a grocery cart. In doing so, they should describe on their activity sheets how their functions would change the cart.

INVENTION FOLLOW-UPS:

There's nothing special about the words listed on the student activity sheet. Additional or different words could be used for improving things. Encourage students to select at random 4 or 5 words from a dictionary and try this activity with a chair, bicycle, or almost anything.

FORGE ~ FITTING FUNCTIONS

Select 3 words from the list below and write them on the dotted lines. Next, write a function or a definition for the 3 words.

radar   foresight   document   estimate   leadership   bonus   compress

defend   combine   transfer   elastic   transport   decision

mandate   bloat   dispenser   offer   jiggle   pitch   pack   rinse   add

WORDS   FUNCTIONS

. . . . _____

. . . . _____

. . . . _____

Decide how you could improve a GROCERY CART by using all 3 word functions. For example, the function of radar is "radio wave location." How about designing a radio wave shopping list inserted into a mechanism on a cart for locating grocery items?

Describe your improvement here.

_____

_____

_____

_____

_____

_____

_____

_____

OUT OF SIGHT:

INVENTIVE THINKING PROCESS: Inventing

WARMING-UP:

1. Provide this activity as an option to those students who like science fiction.

2. Go over the meanings of the word, "REPULSE": (to drive back; repel). Also go over the meanings of the word, "REPULSION": (1. the act of repulsing, or the condition of being repulsed. 2. extreme aversion or dislike).

IDEAS FOR THE DRAWING BOARD:

1. Have students react to the concept of reducing the force of gravity. What kinds of changes would occur on earth if the force of gravity was reduced by 50%?

2. Have students speculate about the use of gravity as a fuel source for transporting space travelers. Where would the "fueling stations" be?

3. Encourage students to imagine how a gravitational repulsion system might work. What advantages would there be for interplanetary travel? How about travel on earth?

4. Should more space be needed for the log entry, have students use the back of their activity sheets.

INVENTION FOLLOW-UPS:

1. Encourage student investigation into the nineteenth century dreams of French author Jules Verne (which have since become realities).

2. Encourage reports on the writings of Isaac Asimov and Ray Bradbury. Have students making the reports speculate on the ideas of these writers and how these ideas might become realities in the twenty-first century.

3. Look for and display artists' conceptions of the future.

"Education for creativity is nothing short of education for living."

Erich Fromm

Invent a GRAVITY REPULSION MODULE. Draw and label the parts.

Enter the events of a Martian's Day in the GRM log.

LOG BOOK

SIMILAR OPPOSITES:

INVENTIVE THINKING PROCESS: Reversing

WARMING-UP:

1. Encourage students to describe a situation in which they felt both happy and sad at the same time.

2. Tell students that at times there are situations to which a pair of opposite words might apply.

IDEAS FOR THE DRAWING BOARD:

1. Have students explain this comment from a visitor at an art gallery, "This is valuable trash." Explain that the words "valuable" and "trash" are words of reversed meanings, but when combined they offer a very descriptive explanation of the viewer's opinion.

2. Distribute the activity sheets and discuss the directions with your class.

3. Encourage students to write descriptive, interesting sentences.

4. Upon completion, encourage students to share their results.

5. As a class, generate other opposite or reversed combinations. Encourage their use in student writing projects.

INVENTION FOLLOW-UPS:

1. Look for word combinations of opposite meanings to describe a typical situation at school.

2. Brainstorm all of the possible situations in which "unanswered response" might apply.

"Individuals, not institutions, create. Let's devise new methods of identifying, teaching and encouraging potential innovators."

Eric P. Schellin, an attorney specializing in patents,
trademarks and copyrights

Similar Opposites

Using language effectively is an inventive process. Try experimenting with word pairs which have opposite or reversed meanings for vivid and descriptive story-telling.

Put together words like NERVOUS and CALM and think about a situation in which they might apply.

The afternoon sky became black and the land turned silent with the NERVOUS CALM of an approaching storm.

Try it with:

1. Deafening and silent.

    _____

    _____

    _____

    _____

2. Stupid and intelligent.

    _____

    _____

    _____

    _____

3. Now select one of your own.

    _____ and_____

    _____

    _____

    _____

    _____

DESIGN A CYCLE:

INVENTIVE THINKING PROCESS: Designing

WARMING-UP:

1. Ask students what a unicorn and a unicycle have in common. How about biannual and a bicycle or a tripod and a triple or a century and a centipede?

2. Indicate that certain prefixes can tell us much about words. Benjamin Franklin in 1780 invented the bifocal lens. It was just a matter of putting a prefix with a root word. Glenn Curtiss in 1911 designed the first hydroplane. Hydro is a prefix meaning water.

IDEAS FOR THE DRAWING BOARD:

1. Don't necessarily encourage students to create a "centicycle," but explain that it is possible. Do, however, encourage them to think of something unusual in constructing their cycles.

2. Challenge students to come up with something that no one else in the class is likely to think of.

INVENTION FOLLOW-UPS:

1. Share and display all of the student cycles.

2. Challenge students to describe how:

   … a cycle is like a calendar.

   … a cycle is like a rubber band.

3. Challenge students with:

   "Which has the better personality:

   … a bicycle or

   … a tricycle?

   … In what ways is it better?"

   "Which is more important:

   … cycling or

   … recycling?

   … Why?"

Design a Cycle

This is a unicycle.

This is a quadricycle.

Design a CYCLE for a starfish or a spider or a centipede or something clever. Do some investigation and determine what the cycle would be called.

INVENTIVE THINKING PROCESS: Redesigning

WARMING-UP:

1. The Dutch ophthalmologist Herman Snellen devised the eye chart in 1862 to test distance acuity.

    A person who is being tested for distance acuity stands twenty feet from an eye chart and reads as many letters as possible. If all the letters in the first eight lines are read correctly, then distance acuity is considered normal, or 20/20.

2. Ask students to recall experiences of having their eyes examined and reading eye charts.

IDEAS FOR THE DRAWING BOARD:

1. Ask students to suggest reasons why commonly recognized words are not included on eye charts. How reliable would eye charts be with easily recognizable words?

2. Suggest to students that they each pretend to be a CHIEF MARKET DESIGNER for a well-established manufacturer of T-shirts. A major idea within the marketing division is to DESIGN an eye chart with a MESSAGE that could be put on T-shirts. In order to promote sales and have a popular consumer item, it is extremely important to have a message that would appeal to kids.

3. Indicate that the dots on the activity page are to serve as a guide for lettering the message. Students are to make their messages look like eye charts by reducing in size the letters on each successive line. They are to use 8 lines.

INVENTION FOLLOW-UPS:

1. Display eye-chart messages in the room. Encourage a student or two to actually apply this design to a T-shirt using iron-on tape, magic markers, or fabric crayons.

2. Do the same activity concept with "ME-CHARTS." Me-charts contain special information about the person who has designed the chart.

3. Encourage student reports on famous Americans who have overcome the handicap of blindness to achieve success. Recommend the genius of Stevie Wonder as a starter.

4. Comparing the retinas of human beings and owls, different acuities occur. Encourage student investigation as to "why?"

5. Encourage a student to make a report on the field of psychophysics. What is it? What kind of research is occurring in this field?

"I" Charts

Redesign an eye chart so that it includes a message.

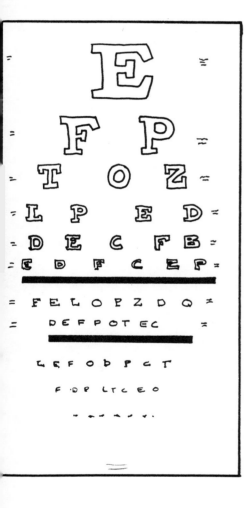

. . . .

. . . .

. . . .

. . . .

. . . .

. . . .

. . . .

. . . .

THE UNWORD STORY: Teacher Directions

INVENTIVE THINKING PROCESS: Finding New Uses

WARMING-UP:

1. Go over the meanings of comic strip symbols with your class.

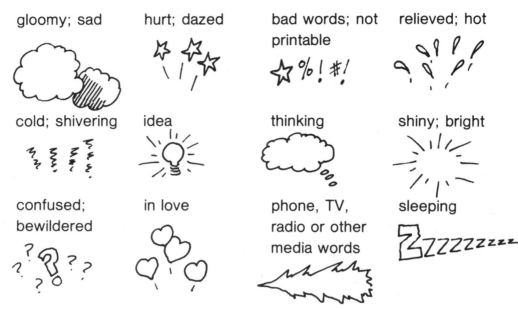

gloomy; sad   hurt; dazed   bad words; not printable   relieved; hot

cold; shivering   idea   thinking   shiny; bright

confused; bewildered   in love   phone, TV, radio or other media words   sleeping

2. Ask for additional symbols from students.

IDEAS FOR THE DRAWING BOARD:

1. Ask students to explain the possible story beginning in the first two frames on their activity page. Encourage many different interpretations.

2. Have students complete the story by using only symbols.

3. Encourage students to create characters for their stories. Discuss character possibilities such as people, animals, ants, termites, flies, aliens, plants, objects, etc.

4. Upon completion, encourage students to display and interpret their stories for the entire class.

INVENTION FOLLOW-UPS:

1. Show a documentary film on well-known world personalities, leaving the sound off. Have student interpret the use of nonverbal communication (hand gestures, posture, etc.,) by the personalities shown.

2. List common forms of nonverbal communication in the classroom, for example, a student who isn't sure of an answer but will raise his/her hand anyway - but in a limp fashion.

3. Display and discuss political satire cartoons and how artists will emphasize certain characteristics of persons and events to convey a point of view.

THE UNWORD STORY

Complete this story by using comic strip symbols. Create your own comic strip characters.

IMPROVE A SMILE:

INVENTIVE THINKING PROCESS: Improving

WARMING-UP:

1. Invention applies to almost anything. There is inventive comedy which enables us to escape from the tensions and stresses of daily living. This activity focuses on improving a very basic human event - a smile. By knowing the things that cause us to see the humor in things or to feel good about things, we can gain a healthier perspective on ourselves and the events that are attempting to shape our lives.

2. Have a discussion on the importance of humor. What is the function of humor? What is the function of a smile?

IDEAS FOR THE DRAWING BOARD:

1. Smiles are reactions to feelings and events. Sometimes we all laugh at the same event. But because we are individuals, often what is funny or pleasurable to one person may not be to another.

2. Encourage students to think of pleasant things, of funny things that through their own experiences would cause them to smile.

3. Advise students to list concise statements and not lengthy descriptions of events on their activity sheets.

4. Knowing what makes an individual smile is worth knowing. Encourage the sharing of comments from the completed activity sheet.

INVENTION FOLLOW-UPS:

1. Provide information or a film about old Charlie Chaplin comedy movie routines. Critics have referred to his routines as being inventive. What makes comedy inventive?

2. Discuss famous comics today. What are their styles and why is it easier for them to criticize government and social issues than for those in other professions?

3. What were the functions of court jesters? Do a current events segment by having students imagine that they are court jesters. Discuss listening comprehension from this type of presentation as compared with a normal presentation. Why does the comedic presentation cause better listening and comprehension?

1. List all the ways you can think of to cause a smile.

_____

_____

_____

_____

_____

_____

_____

_____

_____

2. Which 3 ways would work best for you?

_____

_____

_____

_____

A BAD-TASTE DETECTOR:

INVENTIVE THINKING PROCESS: Inventing

WARMING-UP:

1. Encourage students to state the foods they don't like. Ask if there are ways that a "bad" taste can be determined before tasting something?

2. Have students speculate on other things besides certain foods that taste "bad," for example, envelope glue, medicine, certain mouthwashes, etc.

3. Ask, "How much does odor affect what we eat or taste?" "How about the way something looks?" "What makes something appear appetizing?"

IDEAS FOR THE DRAWING BOARD:

1. Discuss the possible functions of a bad-taste detector. What particular tastes would it detect? What particular smells or colors or shapes or textures would need to be detected?

   Would it be more desirable for it to be a carry-with-you item or something to store in the kitchen.

   How might it function as a detector? Could it be regulated to a person's tastes? Could it be programmed to function for determining too much sugar, too much salt? Could it function to regulate diets? In what ways?

2. After discussion, have students list on their activity sheets the functions they'd like to include for a bad-taste detector. They should rank order the functions on a 1st choice, 2nd choice, 3rd choice, etc., basis.

3. Encourage students to imagine how a bad-taste detector might look if their top 3 functions were to be included.

4. Have them design a detector and label those parts which show the functions.

INVENTION FOLLOW-UPS:

1. Bring (or have a student bring) a smoke detector to school. Discuss the advantages for home and office use.

2. Bring a "strip" thermometer to school. Discuss the advantages of a detector of this type. Investigate "detectors" utilized in surgical rooms, military defense systems and in agriculture.

A Bad-Taste Detector

1. Make up a list of functions for a bad-taste detector.

_____

_____

_____

_____

_____

_____

_____

_____

_____

_____

_____

Rank the functions according to their importance. Write a 1 by the most important; 2 by the second most important; 3 by the third most important.

2. Draw your detector in the space below. Include the most important functions in your drawing.

A LOOK INSIDE:

INVENTIVE THINKING PROCESS: Reversing

WARMING-UP:

1. This exercise calls for "internal visualization" which is an important skill in problem solving. Recognizing the hidden aspects of a problem often leads to finding a solution. Select a house that everyone in your class would recognize, perhaps one across the street from your school, and ask students to describe what they think the house would be like on the inside. Have them describe the locations of bedrooms, kitchen, living room, etc.

2. Ask students to describe the inside of their mouths-the tongue, tonsils, teeth, etc.

3. Challenge students to draw a rough sketch (without looking) of the inside of their lockers or desks. Have them list what books and other materials are where. Have them check it out individually at some later time for accuracy.

IDEAS FOR THE DRAWING BOARD:

1. Upon distribution of the activity sheets, draw attention to the various external parts of the machine, the crank, the receptacle to place things in, the gears, the tap, the nozzle, etc. Encourage students to individually visualize what would be inside. Have them draw the inside and label the parts. It is suggested that an overview drawing be made - much like the interior of a house plan.

2. Have students list what they could place in the machine and what could come out of the machine.

3. Share drawings and ideas.

INVENTION FOLLOW-UPS:

1. Since "internal visualization" was necessary to complete this exercise, have students visualize and describe all of the things that could cause the machine NOT to operate.

2. Encourage students to describe what uses the machine might have if the nozzle were removed.

3. Have students list combinations of things that could be placed in the machine for new and different solutions and mixtures.

A LOOK INSIDE

Draw the internal or inside workings of this machine.

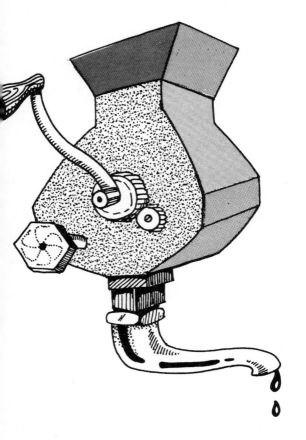

Things to put in:

_____

_____

_____

_____

_____

_____

Things that come out:

_____

_____

_____

_____

_____

_____

DESIGN A PLAYGROUND:

INVENTIVE THINKING PROCESS: Designing

WARMING-UP:

1. Ask students how they might use junkyard things to build a playground.

2. Ask students what kinds of games they could devise for throw-away tires.

3. Ask students if the most expensive things assure "having fun."

IDEAS FOR THE DRAWING BOARD:

1. Encourage students to think about the "perfect" school playground. Have students think about a playground that also serves as a learning resource center. How might ponds, trees and hills be used?

2. How might the principles of conservation serve a school playground?

3. How might playground equipment be built rather than bought? How might other things be put to other uses - like what things could function as a swing or a monkey bar?

4. How large would the ideal playground be?

5. Before beginning the activity, tell students they may want to use map symbols of their own invention to help describe their designs.

6. Provide time for students to describe their ideal school playgrounds and the most interesting elements of them. Have students describe what the functions of their playgrounds are.

INVENTION FOLLOW-UPS:

1. Have a landscape expert talk to your class about landscape design.

2. What are the design elements of a Japanese garden? Encourage a student report on this subject.

3. Design a plan for an outside ecology section on the school playground. Then create it!

4. Ask a civic organization for help in improving your school playground. Old throw-away truck tires and railroad ties and scrap lumber can be turned into exciting innovative playground equipment.

DESIGN A PLAYGROUND

N

PLAYGROUND MAP

Design a school playground you'd really enjoy!

Things on my playground that would make it better than most:

_____

_____

_____

_____

STRETCH A DOUGHNUT:

INVENTIVE THINKING PROCESS: Redesigning

WARMING-UP:

1. Ask how many students have ever seen themselves in a distorted mirror. Indicate that in today's activity you will be visualizing things by distorting their shapes.

2. Tell students that everyday objects have surfaces whose topologies fit certain genuses. For example, genus 0 is a sphere, a cube or an irregular blob. Everyday genus 0 objects might include a football, an orange, a baseball and a banana.

    Genus 1 has a surface with one hole like a doughnut. A vase with a handle, a phonograph record, the numeral 9, the letters A and R are a few examples.

    Genus 2 is a two-holed figure. The letter B, eyeglasses and a two-handled pot are genus 2 figures.

    Genus 3 is a three or more-holed figure. Objects like Swiss cheese, a pretzel, a telephone receiver, a pipe holder for 3 or more pipes would all fit genus 3.

IDEAS FOR THE DRAWING BOARD:

1. Draw attention to the illustration that shows the transformation of a doughnut to a coffee cup. Tell students to imagine how a doughnut might be distorted or twisted in various ways to form a different object. For example, by squeezing the doughnut in the center of the outside perimeter, two holes will appear (genus 2). The two holes might suggest eyeglasses or a candlestick holder.

2. Tell students to visualize the twisting and stretching of a doughnut. When the design of a different object appears, have them jot down the object on scratch paper.

3. Encourage students to sketch on the activity sheet three or four items they redesigned from a doughnut.

INVENTION FOLLOW-UPS:

1. Have a student investigate the Mobius strip and demonstrate the concept of a one-sided surface (Augustus Ferdinand Mobius, 1790-1868).

2. Classify surfaces of objects in a classroom according to genus.

Stretch a Doughnut

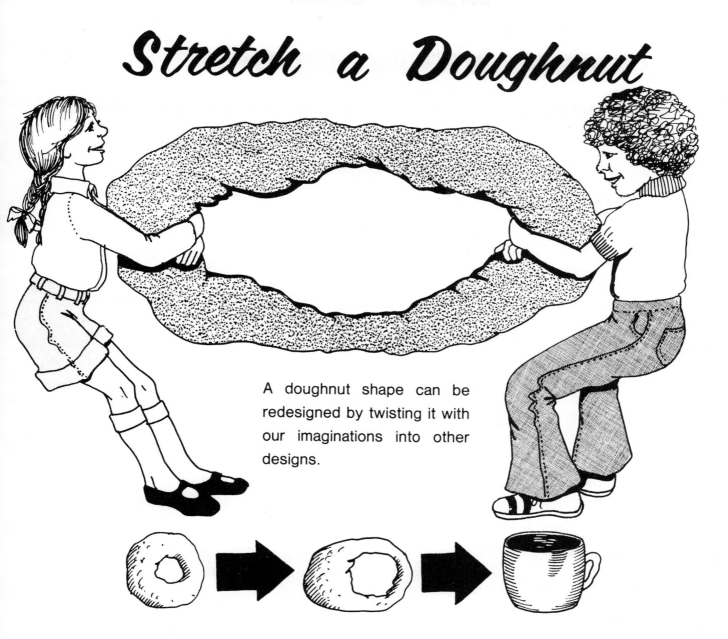

A doughnut shape can be redesigned by twisting it with our imaginations into other designs.

Draw some everyday objects that a redesigned doughnut could be.

THINGS WITHIN THINGS:

INVENTIVE THINKING PROCESS: Finding New Uses

WARMING-UP:

1.   Ask students if they can recall looking at something and seeing something else. Sometimes in wallpaper or in the grain of wood, or in clouds or in shadows we see other objects.

2.   Encourage students to suggest designs that are similar in different products. For example, a razor sort of looks like a vacuum cleaner; an electrical outlet plug looks like the nose of a pig.

IDEAS FOR THE DRAWING BOARD:

1.   Distribute the activity sheet and allow students a day or more to complete the assignment.

   Encourage them to look at things in school, at home, in magazines, etc., for ideas.

2.   Challenge them to come up with something really different — something no one else in the class is likely to do.

3.   Indicate that there are really very few designs in the world that are unique. What we do have are modifications of squares and circles. Sometimes it takes a little patience and study to see the relationship of designs to other designs.

INVENTION FOLLOW-UPS:

1.   Take the letter "Z" and the numeral "7" and arrange them in a design to show a sunburst of arrows.

2.   Look in magazines for corporation logos. Determine the symbolic message of these logos — the message within the message.

3.   Develop "mazes" that contain an inner message.

4.   Thomas Edison had 1,093 patents on inventions. Among his inventions are the electric light, a mimeograph machine, a motion-picture camera and projector, and the phonograph. Encourage a committee of students to investigate as many of Edison's inventions as they can. Have them list the similarities of design within his inventions.

"Every great advance in science has issued from a new audacity of imagination."

John Dewey

THINGS WITHIN THINGS

A paper clip?

Or... A horn?

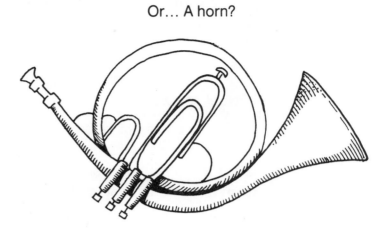

A reversed 7 and a regular 7 or . . .

Shove them together for an arrow.

You think of something within something and draw it below.

INVENTIVE THINKING PROCESS: Improving

WARMING-UP:

1. This exercise deals with the generation of ideas on a very abstract concept. It also deals with the construction of a criterion by which a "best choice" is selected.

2. Improving on anything, be it a feeling or something very concrete, is best accommodated by making choices. Ask students what the world would be like if the only improvement in things would be the things we buy. Ask them to name the unpurchasable improvements.

IDEAS FOR THE DRAWING BOARD:

1. Tell students that a FEELING is something we cannot touch, taste, smell, hear or see, but is a thing that governs what we do and how well we do it.

2. Explain that feelings are very important. How we feel about ourselves is important and how others feel about us is important, too. Sometimes our behavior towards others can make people feel troubled or bad. Sometimes how we really feel is misinterpreted by our actions or lack of actions. *We can be inventive in the way we express our feelings to others* as we can be inventive in improving anything.

3. Without further fanfare, distribute the activity and allow plenty of time for completion.

4. Questions will probably arise as to "What is the function of love?" Use this teachable moment to brainstorm the function of love or "In what ways is love important to us as individuals?"

5. Encourage students to select or adapt some of the brainstormed responses to fit their definitions of love's function. Encourage combining responses to more completely define a student's concept of function.

6. Go back to the activity questions: "If you could choose only one way, which way would you choose?" Ask students to discuss the reasons they chose the items they did. List some of those reasons on the chalkboard. Explain that the reasons represent a criterion by which a choice was made among choices. Explain that in solving problems of any kind, it is extremely important to establish a criterion by which a choice can be made.

INVENTION FOLLOW-UPS:

Encourage students to draw "squiggles" of feeling words like confusion, hate, happiness and embarrassment. Squiggles are abstract formations of lines.

UV

If you couldn't speak or write "I love you" to mom or dad or someone else, in what ways could you show them?

_____

_____

_____

_____

_____

_____

_____

_____

_____

_____

_____

_____

_____

_____

_____

_____

_____

If you could choose only one way,

which way would you choose?

Check ✔ it.

What is the function of love?

WHAT A NAME!   Teacher Directions

INVENTIVE THINKING PROCESS: Inventing

WARMING-UP:

1. Inventions come about by determining what kinds of functions fulfill a need. Students in this activity will analyze a couple of far-out concepts which could fulfill a diversity of functions. The purpose of this exercise is to intellectually diverge on invention functions.

2. Many city libraries will have in their title indexes a number of books listed under "inventions." Some of these books will feature illustrations of inventions from the 1800's to the turn of the twentieth century. Many of these inventions are rather humorous and border on the ridiculous, but they were created to serve specific kinds of functions during that period of time. If available, it is suggested that some of these books be checked out and the illustrations displayed to students. Encourage students to list the functions of some of these inventions.

IDEAS FOR THE DRAWING BOARD:

1. Have a discussion on the advantages of the phone illustrated on the activity sheet. In what ways would a person with a hearing defect benefit from such an invention? How would a telephone of this type function for a person who is absentminded? In what ways might it function for a dentist?

2. How might the shoes function as a wallpaper hanger? How about for a basketball team? How about for catching frogs? What are some other functions ?

3. After generating a few ideas, encourage students to independently list on their activity sheets other functions for the two inventions.

4. Encourage students to name each invention based upon the most important function it serves.

INVENTION FOLLOW-UPS:

1. Do a student count on the total number of different functions cited by the class for each invention. This number should be somewhat surprising.

2. Try the functioning approach in helping students understand why they study what they study. In other words, what is the function of mathematics? What is the function of reading? This is also a good technique for curriculum revision and for stirring up heated discussion in faculty meetings: What is the function of teaching? What is the function of supervision? What is the function of administration? What is the function of parenting?

WHAT A NAME!

Invent some names for these inventions and describe their functions.

_____

_____

_____

_____

_____

_____

_____

_____

_____

_____

_____

_____

REVERSING MYSELF: Teacher Directions

INVENTIVE THINKING PROCESS: Reversing

WARMING-UP:

1. Self-improvement can be an inventive process. Improvement deals, in part, with reversing the way things are in order to gain a greater degree of performance or acceptance of self.

2. Before beginning this activity, have students sit quietly and just think about things they are able to do this year but couldn't do as well two years ago. Provide about 5 minutes of silent contemplation.

IDEAS FOR THE DRAWING BOARD:

1. There are several ways this activity can be done.

   ... One way is to do an anonymous rendition of it by asking students to tear the activity sheet into single statement items. (Do the "I was" statement section apart from the "Now I'm" statement section.) Collect the strips of paper and read at random all of the statements. Follow the reading with a discussion on the importance of improvement and the need to change to accommodate development and growth.

   ... Another way is to have a class discussion, using the "NOW" statements for dealing with aspirations and goals.

   ... Still another way is to simply collect the papers and provide individual conferences. The statements would provide the format.

   The best way to use this activity will be determined by your knowledge of your students.

2. Discuss the concept of a "checklist" for the second half of the activity sheet. "How do we know when we're at the level of performance or achievement we want to be?"

   Ask for a student volunteer to share aloud one of his/her statements. Take the item and brainstorm with the class some possible ways to determine when the level of performance has been met. Begin with the statement, "In what ways would I know when ...." As a class, select the five best suggestions and write them on the chalkboard as a checklist.

INVENTION FOLLOW-UPS:

Have students prepare a list of functions for themselves ten years from now. Begin with,"Ten years from now I'd like to function in the following ways..." Ask students to respond in writing to, "How do I want my friends to function with me?" Have students share papers with a friend.

100

REVERSING MYSELF

Reversing things can be a means of improving things. To see what you've reversed in yourself, try a few of these statements.

I was_____

but now I'm_____

I was_____

but now I'm_____

I was_____

but now I'm_____

Place a ✓ by the item you consider to be the greatest improvement.

Now try it with some NOW statements.

Now I'm _____

but I'd like to be _____

Now I'm _____

but I'd like to be _____

Now I'm _____

but I'd like to be _____

Place a ✓ by the item you consider to be the greatest challenge.

THIS IS MY BAG:

INVENTIVE THINKING PROCESS: Designing

WARMING-UP:

1. Before beginning this activity, have students bring grocery sacks to class. A few additional sacks will be needed for making handle strips. See student activity sheet.

2. Also, before beginning, have magic markers or tempera paint available.

IDEAS FOR THE DRAWING BOARD:

1. Discuss the popular meaning of the phrase, "THIS IS MY BAG."

2. Distribute copies of the student activity sheet and encourage students to think about and list some of their favorite things. Encourage thinking by suggesting hobbies, sports, colors, flowers, school subjects, friends, food, etc.

3. Allow time for the completion of the project. The directions on the student activity sheet should be adequate.

4. Encourage students, upon completion, to list all of the functions for this product that they can. The back of the activity sheet should be used for spill-over responses.

5. As a class, list categories for the functions. In other words, categories might include: time-saving, organizing school things to take home, convenient way(s) to get gym clothes to P.E., etc. Have students compare the functions with the categories to determine what would be the most usable functions for their bags.

6. Provide time for students to explain how their symbols reflect who they are as individuals.

INVENTION FOLLOW-UPS:

1. Should some of the bag functions require heavy materials such as books, suggest that an inner-lining bag be used for additional support.

2. Use a similar approach for organizing room materials. Have "This Is My Bag" learning resources for easy accessibility.

"The human mind is our fundamental resource."

President John F. Kennedy, message to
Congress on the state of U.S. Education,
February 20, 1961

THIS IS MY BAG

Some of my favorite things:

_____sunflowers_____

_____

_____

_____

_____

_____

Symbols for favorite things:

_____

_____

_____

_____

_____

_____

Get a couple of grocery sacks, one for the handles and one for the bag. Cut out two strips of sack paper about 14 × 3 inches. Fold each strip 3 times lengthwise; then "V" the corners. Do the same with the other strip. Staple the handles to the sack.

This is the way you "V" the corners:

Decorate your bag with your symbols and name in a design that pleases you. Print "THIS IS MY BAG" on your bag.

Describe below how your bag would function for you.

SCROODLES:

INVENTIVE THINKING PROCESS: Redesigning and Finding New Uses

WARMING-UP:

1. A scroodle is a type of noodle which has a spiral design. Using the idea of a spiral, students will be asked to add things to a scroodle design in order to create something novel and interesting.

2. Before beginning the activity, ask students to describe what a droodle is and under what circumstances people would draw them.

IDEAS FOR THE DRAWING BOARD:

1. After distributing the activity, encourage students to look at the examples. Indicate that in the first example a scroodle can be imagined to be almost anything. Encourage students to speculate on how a scroodle lasso might be drawn.

2. For additional humor and motivation, ask students if they can imagine what song might be appropriate as the national anthem for scroodles. Render a few stanzas of "Old MacDonald Had a Farm," and when you get to the e--i, e--i--o chorus, point out that these letters when written in a certain style look like scroodles.

3. Upon completion of the activity sheets, enjoy the creative responses of student scroodles.

4. Doing scroodles is a good exercise in creative expression since a structure has been provided which promotes flexible thinking — that is, thinking across categories of thought.

INVENTION FOLLOW-UPS:

1. On the back of the activity sheets, encourage students to draw "ringlets" or "squiggles" or "squares" or "triangular" scroodles and provide lines for an addition or two. Give this variation a title, too.

2. Ask students to identify everyday scroodles, for example, a telephone wire or a twisted garden hose, etc.

3. Ask what the functions of scroodles are. What if all the scroodles in the world became squiggles?

Scroodles

Redesign a scroodle by adding things to it.

This is a scroodle.

This is a "SCHOONER ON A SCROODLE."

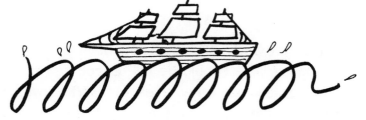

This is a "SCROODLE CHORUS " or "SCROODLE POODLES."

Now do two scroodles of your own and give each a title.

This is _____

This is _____

FIELD GOAL MACHINE:

INVENTIVE THINKING PROCESS: Finding New Uses

WARMING-UP:

1. Have students explain the function of a field goal kicker in the game of football.

2. Ask students to imagine how a practice session might be conducted by a field goal kicker.

IDEAS FOR THE DRAWING BOARD:

Tell students you hope Bert makes the team, but it is essential that he think of some other possibilities should he fail. Encourage students to list as many ideas as possible on other uses for Bert's invention. Also, tell students to list ideas that might call for a slight redesign of the invention. For instance, it could be used, with an alteration to the conveyor belt system, as a device for teeing balls on a golf driving range.

INVENTION FOLLOW-UPS:

1. Have students check ✓ on the illustrated activity sheet all of the possible malfunctions on Bert's machine. Each area of possible malfunction would, of course, be a function. How might functions be combined to reduce possible malfunctions? In what ways would the machine be improved by doing this?

2. Encourage students to design a better machine.

3. Encourage students to identify machines associated with athletics and how these machines assist athletes in improving their skills.

4. Investigate how computers are improving athletic skills.

"To set the stage . . . for the steady support of creative manifestations in any child, youth, or adult, our schools should get beyond the dull, the safe, the orthodox. Any excitement lost to our schools will be lost to our communities ten times over."

George D. Stoddard

FIELD GOAL MACHINE

Bert wants a tryout with a pro team as a field goal kicker. He invented this machine to help him practice.

If Bert fails in his tryout, how might he put his machine to other uses?

packaging grapefruit, oranges, apples, etc.

_____

_____

_____

_____

_____

_____

_____

_____

SUCTION CRITTER:

INVENTIVE THINKING PROCESS: Improving

WARMING-UP:

Indicate to students that, at times, scientific invention comes about from some very unusual sources. For instance, in the comic strip, "Dick Tracy," the 2-way radio wristwatch was worn by Tracy long before an actual application was made from the idea. In all probability, the old comic strip, "Buck Rogers," may have a similar coincidence with space technology of the future.

IDEAS FOR THE DRAWING BOARD:

1. Encourage students to observe carefully the illustration on the activity sheet. "What's coming out of the critter's ears?"

2. Have students complete the activity page. Their observations of the critter should provide data as to its function. Their imaginations should provide information as to how this critter could improve things.

3. The last question calls for the application of the critter's function to some very difficult problems existing today, such as new energy sources, problems of recycling materials, storage of nuclear waste, etc.

4. Provide time for students to explain their inventions and how they would function for the improvement of things.

INVENTION FOLLOW-UPS:

1. Discuss the problems of using resources and ecology, especially in those areas in which they are not compatible.

2. Discuss the potential "waste" problem in space.

3. Discuss energy usage from waste materials.

"Creativity is the encounter of the intensively conscious human being with his world."

Rollo May

SUCTION CRITTER

1. This is a suction critter. How does it function?

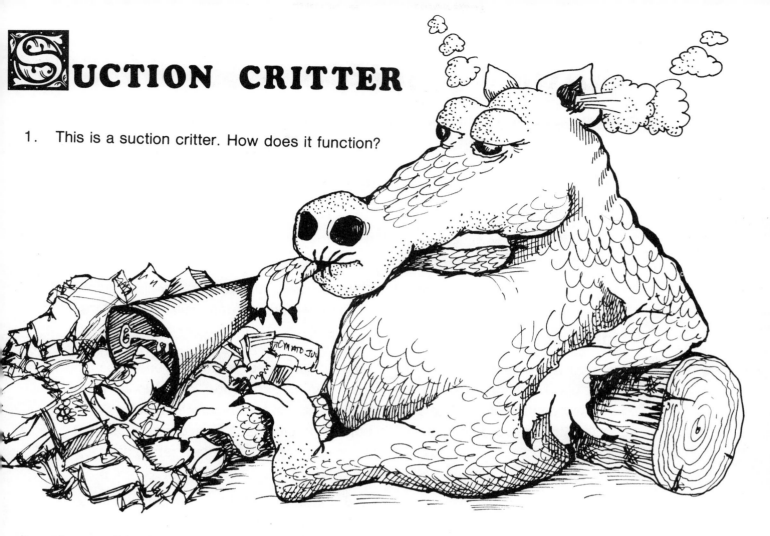

2. How could it function to improve things?

3. If the suction critter became a machine, what might it look like?

COLOR MY SPEECH:

INVENTIVE THINKING PROCESS: Inventing

WARMING-UP:

1. This exercise deals with using a structured format for generating new, unusual and inventive student-written responses.

2. Ask students to describe how the language of popular novelists differs from the written style of most ordinary writers in nonnovelist professions.

IDEAS FOR THE DRAWING BOARD:

1. Have students, upon receiving the activity sheet, complete each column fully before attempting the next column. Encourage students to write words or phrases that come to mind and not to concern themselves with matching words or phrases in adjoining columns. You might suggest that students cover a completed column with a piece of paper before attempting the next one.

2. When the columns are completed, students should create combinations as cited in the example on the activity sheet. Encourage students to write only those combinations that most appeal to them. Should more space be needed, encourage use of the back side of the activity sheet for additional statements.

3. Call upon students to share their statements with the total class.

INVENTION FOLLOW-UPS:

1. Encourage students to change the order of columns for a different approach and meaning.

2. Create different column headings for variation of creative expression.

3. Encourage the expansion of a statement into a paragraph or even a short story.

4. Encourage students to compile a list of expressive statements for future use in developing their own creative writing skills.

COLOR MY SPEECH

Colorful or picturesque language is a product of inventive thinking.
Try it with this exercise.

Write a 2-word descriptive phrase about anything:	Write something you can see from a car window:	List an object or thing you can't touch:
1. calm stillness	1. OF A	1. IS LIKE
2.	2. OF A	2. IS LIKE a promise
3.	3. OF A wheatfield	3. IS LIKE
4.	4. OF A	4. IS LIKE
5.	5. OF A	5. IS LIKE
6.	6. OF A	6. IS LIKE
7.	7. OF A	7. IS LIKE

Match any words in columns one, two and three for an original and inventive statement. Write your best combinations here.

The calm stillness of a wheatfield is like a promise.

_____

_____

_____

_____

_____

_____

_____

_____

PART IV:
LESSON PLANNING FOR INVENTIVE THINKING

Inventive thinking should be a continuing process because it promotes life-application skills. There are a number of things that can easily be integrated within any curriculum to nurture intellectual inventiveness. What follows are some 100 suggestions for doing just that.

1. Doing fun-to-do writing topics, such as "Make up a story about how sloths got their feet with three toes."

2. Brainstorming definitions to fit a poetic structure like haiku or cinquain. Make up a poem about "tenderness" using words brainstormed from "What is tenderness?" Use selected words to fit the poetic structure.

3. Combining functions, such as "Think of something on a string. Think of something good to eat and use your imagination in joining the two things together. How would they function together?"

4. Adding functions: "What extraordinary functions might a textbook perform in helping one study?"

5. Rearranging information or withholding information in order to promote student inquiry.

6. Using imaginary words in order to generate imaginative fantasy: "Draw a kangaroonie."

7. Encouraging multiple explanations or hypotheses for discrepant events after providing events that are discrepant.

8. Playing with improbabilities, such as "What would happen if man's life expectancy was 500 years?"

9. Writing funny similes.

10. Finding out what's in a closed box without opening it.

11. Looking at things from different perspectives: "Describe the inside of a dragon." "Be an atom and write about your relationship with an overbearing molecule." "Draw a cross section of something you can't break in half."

12. Doing time capsule perceptions of yourself: "Pretend you could place 5 things (to describe you), other than photographs, in a time capsule. What would you select?"

13. Asking, "What is the function of . . .?"

14. Expanding application of learned skills: "How many verbs would describe the hitting of a golf ball?" Expect answers like slice, shank, bogied, parred, drive, tap, pulled, pitched, eagles, birdied, chipped, etc.

15. Doing sociodramas.

16. Determining the number of ways to do, look at, or change something.

17. Doing comparisons, such as "A loud siren sounds like ...... because both can ...... and ...... " or "A willow tree is like an umbrella because ...."

18. Adding fun to the basic skills by doing some variations with grammar: "Which is the best swimmer - swim, swam or swum?" Also try it with, "Which takes up more room - a conjunction or a preposition?" Be sure to ask why.

19. Asking for the invention of unconventional things, such as a "sneeze-squeezer."

20. Doing creative movement to music, to words, or something still, such as a painting.

21. Providing provocative or absurd situations and asking for logical explanations. Providing logical situations and asking for provocative or absurd explanations.

22. Dealing with the future: "What it would be like traveling by conveyor belt or taking a weekend jaunt to the moon?"

23. Expanding the notion of things: "If you were blue, what could you be?"

24. Showing expression of human emotions through photographs and asking students to think of all the things they can that would cause a particular expression.

25. Trying word drills, such as "How many different things could you buy at a grocery store with the same sound as the sound in your name?"

26. Expanding the uses of things: "How many different uses are there for a smudge of peanut butter?"

27. Using sensory approaches, such as giving a marshmallow to students to feel, squeeze, smell and taste. Discuss the properties and relate those properties to other things.

28. Beginning discussion and assignment topics with the words "Just suppose . . ."

29. Using puppets and other stimuli for fantasy explorations in order to gain information about something.

30. Doing creative dramatics for understanding historical events.

31. Reversing order. Tell students that an answer is "rough and scratchy." Ask them to write some questions. Try it with things academic. The answer is "friction." Write some questions.

32. Accommodating perceptual viewing. Provide a design and ask, "How many different things can you see?"

33. Thinking in terms of other uses: "What can you do with a newspaper besides read it?"

34. Studying the social sciences with personal-involvement techniques and the past with time-machine techniques.

35. Promoting problem sensitivity: "Suppose you were 2 inches high. List different things that might occur to you."

36. Using open-ended topics for writing and research topics.

37. Thinking in terms of alternatives: "How many different ways could you go to school?" Thinking in terms of solution-finding: "Which would be

the best way to school on a rainy day? What if you have a broken foot? What if you also have a lot of books to carry?"

38. Creating sensitivity to life: "What if your best friend were a saltwater fish?"

39. Taking a word (such as the word "bird,") and listing all the other words that come to mind.

40. Placing an invisible creature in an empty chair and providing a few clues. Have students draw a picture of the creature based upon the clues provided.

41. Identifying problems and beginning the problem statement with "In what ways can I . . . ?"

42. Asking for the possible consequences of any real or imagined event: "What changes in the world would occur if India were turned upside down?"

43. Combining the attributes of one object with those of another object to find a new object.

44. Accommodating "novelty" approaches to conventional dilemmas.

45. Asking a lot of "What might happen?" questions.

46. Challenging students to come up with unusual things, such as "Create a recipe for aardvark pudding."

47. Nurturing observation skills — perhaps by inviting the principal into the classroom for a 3-second stay. After departure have students list individually what color of clothes, personal effects, etc., the principal wore.

48. Making up better book titles, song titles and newspaper headlines for current books, songs and articles.

49. Accommodating critical thinking by having "critical reviews" of current television programs that will be watched regardless of events.

50. Trying word-awareness activities such as acrostics (vertical words within a column of words) or anagrams (rearrange letters in one word to form another word).

51. Creating "punctuation" sounds for oral reading of short statements, rhymes or quotations.

52. Using analogies for a greater understanding of something.

53. Doing classroom dioramas with only natural materials (bark, snake skins, etc.).

54. Encouraging student readings as though the events were really happening to the reader.

55. Giving four or five letters and having students generate as many words as possible within a determined time frame (for example, 3 minutes).

56. Encouraging the design of different experiments to test the same principle.

57. Trying metaphorical associations: "Describe the emotions of a window or a mirror." Forcing associations of anything that appears unrelated to something.

58. Rank-ordering events: "What would happen if we had no rain for a year?" "What would happen if there were no employment?"

59. Personifying objects that don't work: "If I were a lock, how many different things could go wrong with me and keep me from working?"

60. Synthesizing: "What could you make shorter to make it last longer?"

61. Creating different story endings to well-known stories.

62. Using colors to paint feelings.

63. Writing "experience" definitions to phrases: "Eerie is . . ." "Small is . . ."

64. Using different frames-of-reference, such as looking at gasoline prices through the eyes of a traveling salesman or looking at a junkyard through the eyes of a sculptor or a land developer.

65. Transposing the senses: "In what ways can warmth be seen or in what ways can a feeling be heard?"

66. Relating to imagery: "What are the tastes and smells of December?"

67. Writing slogans for a make-believe company product.

68. Designing futuristic transportation modes.

69. Creating a magic machine and telling what it would do.

70. Making associations: "What events are similar to a chain of exploding firecrackers?"

71. Dealing with dimensionality: "How many squares can you make by folding a single piece of paper?"

72. Dealing with undimensionality: "When I am sad, I'm like a . . ."

73. Interchanging parts by adding unusual prefixes or suffixes in place of more commonly accepted ones for more meaning and clarity.

74. Determining the properties of different things: "What is the property of a smile?"

75. Finding variations in things: "In what other ways can I use it?"

76. Reversing the operation of something to see what would happen. Try it with music or anything where a sequence of events is involved.

77. Developing nonsensical words to describe human experiences and events: "Describe the blahs, the ickies, the ahaaas."

78. Redesigning designs or creating designs of who we are: "Draw a family crest or a personal logo." "Redesign your room."

79. Dealing with abstractions by drawing splots and squiggles in a way that would define their functions.

80. Improving things. For example, brainstorm different ways to get a group of kids lined up for lunch.

81. Restructuring things, for example, building new shapes from existing forms.

82. Using word functions of unrelated words to improve something.

83. Dealing with issues in a humorous way: "How might an inchworm react to metric conversion?"

84. Dealing with emotional weights: "Which carries more commitment - love or hate?"

85. Finding out how things function upside down: "If you turned the alphabet upside down, what words would still have a function?"

86. Valuing: "If you could read only one book during the rest of your life, what book would you choose?"

87. Weighing degrees: "Which is the worst - cheating on a test, taking something belonging to someone else, hurting someone's feelings, telling a lie for personal gain or taking advantage of someone?"

88. Providing structure to promote creativity, such as writing sentences with one basic word: "Red reddens reddishly the redness."

89. Promoting flexibility and fluency by writing as many different sentences as possible with only six words.

90. Making choices based on functions: "Would you rather be a multiplication table or a dinner table?"

91. Inventing words and defining them: "What is a goomerrang?"

92. Listing things: "List things you like to touch; things you like to think about; things you like to hear."

93. Looking for additional meanings, for instance, using homographs: "Which requires more caution — forks in the road or forks on the table."

94. Describing things: "What ING word would best describe a gnarled old oak tree?"

95. Investigating the causes of the way things are: "Look at a world map and determine what land masses might have been joined at one time. Develop a hypothesis."

96. Discovering ways to calculate things: "List all the ways you can think of to calculate the size and weight of an unseen hippopotamus."

97. Doing two-people poetry readings with advertisements, poems and statements. (Each person takes a line from a different selection.)

98. Writing the history of a community by using only a telephone directory.

99. Determining how many ways something can be divided into four equal parts.

100. Closing the school days with "What did you learn today?"

PART V:
UNCONVENTIONAL INVENTION
PATENT

For achievement in . . .

Challenging assumptions for the improvement of things.

Generating ideas and solutions that are original, unconventional, and unique.

Demonstrating curiosity, persistence and motivation.

Ascertaining the essence of how things function or might function.

Utilizing and reconstructing materials to express an idea.

UNCONVENTIONAL INVENTION PATENT

PATENT NO. _____

TITLE _____

DESCRIPTION _____
_____
_____

NAME OF INVENTOR _____

All rights and privileges are hereby bestowed to the inventor and to this
UNCONVENTIONAL INVENTION.

DATE _____

SEAL

121

THE GROWING FAMILY OF GOOD GP APPLE PRODUCTS AND SERVICES INCLUDES:

5 Periodicals to Meet the Needs of Educators

THE GOOD APPLE NEWSPAPER For grades 2-8. Each issue contains BIG (17½ x 22½) pages filled with creative, easy-to-use ideas. Features include full-size gameboards, seasonal units, reproducible activity pages, and much more. A wealth of ideas coming your way five times each year.

LOLLIPOPS For preschool-grade 2. Each issue provides timely teaching tips and professional articles that help to create a happy classroom environment. A special section of tear-out reproducible activity sheets and special units accompany this popular periodical. *Lollipops* comes your way five times each school year.

CHALLENGE Reaching and teaching the gifted child k-8. Each exciting issue contains a section of easy-to-use, practical and motivating activities. Other features include complete units of study, tips for parents of gifted children, interviews with gifted adults and children and much more. *Challenge* comes your way five times each school year.

OASIS For grades 5-9. *Oasis* contains reproducible activity sheets for all content areas, articles on the most current topics, interdisciplinary units plus much more. *Oasis* is published five times each school year to provide you with a continuous flow of new and exciting ideas.

SHINING STAR An exciting Christian education publication for k-8. Each issue includes motivating ideas, bulletin boards, Bible games, crafts, seasonal activities, reproducible work sheets and more. For use in church, home and school. *Shining Star* is published quarterly.

Good Apple Idea and Activity Books

In all subject areas for all grade levels, preschool-12. Idea books, activity books, bulletin board books, units of instruction, reading, creativity, readiness, gameboards, science, math, social studies, responsibility education, self-concept, gifted, seasonal ideas, arts/crafts, poetry, language arts, and teacher helpers.

Good Apple has just the book you have been looking for

and

Activity Posters • Note Pads • Software • Videos

and there is still more!

Good Apple is also proud to distribute Monday Morning Books. This fine line of educational products includes creativity, arts and crafts, reading, language arts and early learning resources.

Shining Star is a division of Good Apple, Inc. Its products include Christian education material for school, church and home. For grades k-8.

Workshops

Good Apple can provide your school with the workshop to meet your needs. We have a variety of specialists who will design the workshop specifically for your school.

If a school supply store is not available in your area, please write for a FREE catalog to Good Apple, Inc., Box 299, Carthage, IL 62321-0299